Marital Physics

Marital Physics
The Science Of Success In Marriage

IVAN & PAULINE HERALD
© 2015
OzFAME

Contents

Introduction

Life's not static. It's also not always fair. It is constantly filled with the ebb and flow of relational change. Some good, some – well we won't go there. Why is it that so many married couples often fall into the mundane, the ordinary, and the predictable? Nothing in this universe is static. Change is an integral part of life.

If you don't confront change directly and almost intentionally, it will run right over the top of you and your relationship. It's not a matter of adapting to change; it is more confrontation of change that's required.

You might say: *"Not another marriage book." "Hey, what about other relationships?"* Well quite honestly I don't want to waste my time supporting the second of two types of relationships that clearly is not as successful as marriage. My footnotes here may be far too long. I agree. However, currently because of often-unfair bias against marriage, this point of the priority of marriage sadly has to be strongly validated and vigorously defended. No one says 'marriage is perfect,' but marriage surely is a whole lot more successful than de facto relationships[1].

---

1 By 2000 well over half of all first marriage are preceded by cohabitation [Uni. Wisconsin document] Now it is 76% in Australia [ABS].
- Cohabitation doesn't reduce the likelihood of divorce; in fact it leads to a higher divorce rate. One study showed it has a 46% higher risk than the normal divorce rate [1992 Journal of Marriage and the Family].
- No positive contribution of cohabitation to marriage has ever been found, not even sexual compatibility as usually suggested [1993 Journal of Marriage and the Family].
- PLEASE NOTE: Because of the need for extensive reference supporting marriage it was deemed necessary to keep the footnote referencing above brief, and conclude the rest of the references at the end of the book as an 'Endnote.' Kindly consult further supportive material reinforcing the position of marriage at end of book.

De facto partners tragically have a much higher separation rate and termination of the relationship than married couples, often resulting in serial de facto status. That's really great for stability of children isn't it? Also consider that de facto relationships have a much higher incidence of violence in the home, murder of partner, and abuse (verbal, physical, and sexual) of partner and children (especially for the children when the male is not the biological father), than married relationships. So why on earth would I include, support, promote, or attempt to bolster such?

My sole concern in this book is for reinforcing marriages – pure and simple.

Now if I lose readers at this point then I regret their loss. Intelligent, serious-minded individuals will always carefully examine the evidence on both sides of a subject. That's what I'm appealing to – serious-minded individuals who want to see developed the best possible environment for them personally, and the best relationship to raise healthy, well-balanced children. Thus far that environment clearly is a loving marriage!

The Purity Of Physics And Mathematics.

Wouldn't it be good if we could reduce effective, maturing and growing marriages down to a common formula as in physics or mathematics? That would make the life of the couple and the counsellor a lot simpler.

I'm sure we're all aware of the brilliance of Albert Einstein, Isaac Newton, and other great academic brains. In one 'simple' (and we here use that term very advisedly) formula Einstein expressed: ***The Theory Of Relativity***. Most of us know his ingenious formula as:

$$E = mc^2$$

(Even if we haven't got a clue what it means.)

The Theory Of Relativity transformed theoretical physics and astronomy during the 20th century. When first published, relativity theory superseded a 200-year-old 'theory of mechanics' created and originally articulated primarily by Isaac Newton

Let's pretend we could transform an effective marriage to a simple formula. Maybe we can envisage a counsellor sitting with a couple having marriage problems and saying: "Now to get to 'E' (Effective Marriage), you need an 'M' and a 'C,' and you've got it made. Oh goodness, I can see your problem. You've only got one 'C.' You're supposed to have 'C' squared. There's your problem right there. Thank you, that will be $160 for today. See you same time next week?"

Life isn't always about neat formulas. It's rarely 'one size fits all.' We're all individuals, snowflake personalities. But, having said that, let's have some fun with the topic of marriage, formulas, physics and mathematics.

Key Elements In The Book.

I have threaded throughout this work certain key elements that will, I hope, both keep you interested, and provide a useful foil against which to display the priceless jewel of a great marriage. They are:

- The inclusion of some concepts of physics and mathematics from the 'created and factual world' of Isaac Newton. They will 'tease in' the introduction of each of the four Sections in what we trust is an entertaining way. Though all the mathematic and physics principles along with the historical facts referred to are bedded in truth the reader is invited into a hypothetical world of creative imagination for a brief interlude.

- You will meet seven couples throughout the book. They will appear in each of the four Sections to come. We live in a world of 'Reality TV and Media,' though often not much is reality. We want to illustrate our principles of attempting to reach marital bliss through the lives of the seven couples revealed in the pages to come. Some will succeed in their marriage, some will not – just like life. By using real life cases it will humanise our principles.

- We will introduce clinical research that illustrates or amplifies the points we are making. Fortunately, the last forty years has brought a significant and helpful amount of 'tested principles' from the social research clinics of highly trained individuals.[2]

- Challenge to old sayings and old adages. So often we just accept old sayings – eg: 'Absence makes the heart grow fonder.' Ok, I get the point, but actually how accurate is it, especially when applied to modern marriages? Can we review some of these 'old sayings' with an up-to-date eye and an open mind, as they may apply to healthy ongoing relationships? We will use them as a heading and a springboard of thought to each sub-section.

Before commencing we need to in advance apologise to all the mathematicians, physicists, and historical purists. Don't get cross with me if you think I'm stretching the boundaries about the story of Isaac Newton. Just stay with me for the fun of the ride. **All** of the historical details are absolutely accurate. It is the story's application to marriage that has entered into the wondrous realm of 'story-telling.' Isaac Newton's friends are imaginary, the truths however very real. No real harm intended.

The Problem:

One bright spark I was listening to said it was quite ok to have sixteen wives. Now, he definitely had everyone's attention. "Sure it is," he said. "In the marriage ceremony it clearly says you can have 'four richer, four poorer, four better, four worse.'"

Everybody laughed. But, there is the problem in itself. Failing relationships have become so numerous and so painful, that one of the oft-used

---

2 We will try to keep these references brief, unlike No. 1 footnote. On rare occasions however I have not always noted in my extended notes in this work all the source recognition details. In researching I noted some valuable points being raised then was distracted to take down the actual source origin. Sorry about this, but I will still use a limited amount of this reliable none-referenced material.

copping strategies society utilises is to make fun of the subject. That's not a solution, that's escapism. Before we start on the book's 'Four Sections' let's look briefly at the state of marriage.

Does our society really take marriage breakdown seriously? Isn't it more often 'Crisis Management' than 'Preventative Maintenance?' All too often it is 'ambulance at the bottom of the hill' instead of 'ambulance at the top of the hill.'

Dinosaur Bill.

Let's look at Bill for a moment. His entire life and attitudes reflect his marriage. On most weekends, you can find him in his faded oil-stained stubby blue shorts and his greasy blue singlet top (neither of which have been washed for 6 weeks). Barefoot he sits on the edge of the engine housing of his prized classic 1971 General Motors Holden Kingswood car. He's tinkering away at the motor, feet right inside the engine housing. He's been restoring the car for years. One day he'll have her ready. One day!

He wouldn't dare let any oil stain the car's precious and perfect paintwork, so he's 'borrowed' his wife's favourite and special tea towel to sit on. Helen had bought it as a unique souvenir from the Tower of London on their UK trip. And, Bill hasn't got a clue why Helen's upset with him. Right now she'd like to take him to The Tower of London.

Bill hasn't quite caught up with the fact it's the 21stCentury. Today, nobody can sit on the edge of their car's engine housing and stick their feet inside whilst they work on the motor. There's nowhere for your feet amid the three and a half million wires, electronic wizardry and computer chips that all seem to fail one day after the guarantee runs out.

It's not that Bill refuses to embrace a new day and age; he hasn't even realised it's happened. And, its not that someone hasn't tried to help him. Bill's just stubborn. His squealing and digging in of the heels rivalled the pig in the sty getting its throat cut to make the Christmas ham.

Oh, Bill has tried counselling. Once! Looking at Helen he said: "Well, woman if it'll make yur appy I'll give it a go. Maybe yur can learn somethin."

Bill has really missed the point, hasn't he? The session only lasted 20 minutes, before he stormed out furious. Some suggestion by the counsellor about Bill having to check some of his attitudes seemed to enrage him. How odd!

Bill grumbled to himself all afternoon. "Who do they think they are? What's more that counsellor was a 'Sheila.' What are the blokes at the pub gonna think about that?" Not that Bill would dare tell them.

Has Bill always been like this? No. Didn't he once have passion, adventure, and romance? Sure. In his dashing courting days Bill pursued Helen, his bride to be, with perseverance and an energy paralleling exhaustion.

They went to the county fair and had so much fun. With giant fluffy toys tucked under his arm, which he'd won at the rifle shoot, Bill didn't feel any embarrassment coming home with Helen on the train, fluffy toys in tow. Bill took Helen rowing on the lake and walking in the forest. They sat and watched the sun come up across the ocean, after talking all night about what a wonderful life they would have together.

As a couple they giggled chasing each other through the dappled sunlight of the woodlands of the Southern Highlands and fell laughing, in huge piles of coloured leaves, when Helen let him catch her. They threw the red, orange, brown and golden autumn leaves all over each other before happily falling into each other's arms in a huge pile of leaves.

Back then Bill had often bought Helen little gifts from his meagre wage. His love was true and sacrificial.

When Helen raised the issue with Bill of why he didn't do any of those things any more, his answer sent her cold.

"Listen, ya gotta grow up yur know. Can't be stupid all yur life!" Bill turned away annoyed to storm out the back door. He was off to the shed again, off to the Kingswood. Or, was it the cave? He didn't see the tears welling up in Helen's eyes. More sadly Bill wouldn't have cared.

Bill is a dinosaur. He won't face change. Bill won't actively confront change. He doesn't even know what change is.

Change is inevitable for all of us, except from vending machines. He who isn't prepared to change is either perfect to start with, or mighty stubborn thereafter. Bill is stubborn. He actually gives new definition to the term.

Though the statement might smart a little, think about another wise axiom. He, who isn't prepared to change, ends up in chains.

As previously stated wouldn't it be good if a great, enriching and enduring marriage could be expressed as a simple formula? Well maybe it can be to a certain extent. Maybe marriage is as simple or as organised as physics, or a formula.

In this book I want to challenge us all about becoming proactive in confronting change, accepting personal responsibility, and pulling individually our weight. I don't want any of my relationships, most of all my marriage, to end up in chains.

Originally I had thought about giving this book the title of *'Confrontational Marriage,'* but decided that such a title conveyed to some a slightly less than desirable negative connotation, that skim readers may misinterpret, rather than see the deeper implications. Indeed, I do want people to confront in their marriage – but not their spouse! For the most enduring, relationship-building marriage we all need to **confront ourselves**, our own actions, our attitudes, and our personal commitment and contribution to the marriage.

Our sense of responsibility will adjust with time. When children are born such requires a serious rethink on many aspects of how we contribute to our marriage. Sickness, changing home, retirement, and changing employment dynamics also all affect the way we consider, reorganise and share household and marriage responsibilities.

My youngest grandson, Declan, recently assured me of changing responsibilities. It was our grandson's eighth birthday, and we were at the sports oval watching him play soccer. He proudly announced that, following their quaint household tradition; he didn't have to fulfil his general responsibilities that day, seeing it was his birthday.

So Declan was exempt from making his bed, putting his clothes in his drawer from the ironing basket, unpacking the dishwasher, and so on. This cute privilege applied to everyone in their family on their birthday.

I complained to him and said that I didn't get the day off from responsibilities when it was my birthday. I mentioned all the things I would need to do during the day as he patiently listened, not realising I was teasing him into a 'pity-party' for me.

"Don't worry Pa," he quickly responded, "you can have the day off next year, if you're still alive!"

Then he realised what he'd said as his grandmother was in fits of hysterical laughter. Great support, I don't think.

Quickly he added: "Don't worry Pa, I'm not saying you're old. It's just well, we've all got to go sometime."

You don't need to guess very long now at the cause of Pauline's continued, even more hysterical laughter.

Great recovery Declan. Thanks honey I don't think.

Trust I get time to finish this chapter.

What Causes The Death Of Romantic Love?

Two social researchers out of the USA, A. Wood and W. Nimkoff[3] discovered, to the horror of those working with couples that up to 80% of romantic love potentially diminishes in the lives of most couples in the first two years of marriage.

Can we grasp that? Up to 80%!

Remember your courting days. Can you remember the chase, the fun, and the excitement? What happens for many that they don't keep such alive, active, and current?

"Oh, we get old," I hear you say.

Rubbish! Getting old is not the problem. Your attitudes are. And attitude is what life is all about.

We've all seen couples in their 70's and 80's fresh as a daisy, playful with each other, having so much fun, keeping the glow alive. Sure their bodies may move a little slower – but not their hearts.

I challenge you to commit to change. I want to encourage you to become confrontational in your marriage. When I say confrontational, I don't mean

---

3 A Wood; W. Nimkoff 'Courtship and Personality,' American Journal of Sociology, 1948, 53 pp 263-269. Reviewed and cited in Family/Marriage Journals to this date. Though commenced as a 1948 research (with later several research updates) their work constantly remains currently relevant, constantly referred to and reconfirmed by other social therapists and counsellor research.

negative confrontation with your spouse. I mean being positively confrontational with yourself.

Ask yourself: "What am 'I' doing today to build my relationship?" "What am 'I' doing to keep, not only the spark alive, but, the marriage aflame with passion?"

The tragedy with many people is that they embrace change in so many other areas of life, but not in their relationship. As life goes on they upgrade the house. They buy a new car every few years. Keeping up-to-date they will recarpet, refurnish, and acquire the latest electronic white goods and entertainment systems. Constantly most people are upgrading their computers, especially their programs, or hard-drive operations. As life improves, they rethink their holidays with a bit more luxury.

Few people; however, ever upgrade – that is deliberately upgrade – their marriage relationship.

Some issues in life intentionally make us think through change. When children are born we have to rethink our household job's allocation schedule, how we use our time, our money, and engage our social life. In fact for many couples it becomes: "What did I do with my life before this?"

Some physical changes require thought about the change process, like menopause, pregnancy, male mid-life crisis, and andropause. Retirement obviously requires change. However, tragically most people see these as events we must pass through, not anything to do with relational change.

When it comes to many life changes, what are the usual dominant attitudes we hear from people? "You know, you just have to get over it." What nonsense! This was the old way of dealing with such challenges. And, it often didn't work. These challenges should be the zones of deliberate confrontation.

In the last few years, attitudes have seriously changed about how we deal with these predictable life challenges. Are we really going to treat life-challenging issues like a phase we have to get over? That's an out-dated old view.

Or, will we be proactive and use that phase to take the relationship to a new level. We have to accept the responsibility that comes with the challenge, not always making the issue someone else's responsibly – especially our spouse.

Are You Ruled By Primary Or Secondary Reactions?

Let's look for a moment at Sally and James. After four years of extremely happy, blissful, and fun-filled years of marriage they are beside themselves with joy at Sally's pregnancy. It is planned happiness.

When Jeremiah is born, they are ecstatic. However, all is not as it could be for Sally. After a good delivery Sally unfortunately goes into severe post-natal depression. Medical experts say it can occur potentially in up to 20% of women in the Western World. "Postnatal depression affects around 15% of all child-bearing women" in Australia.[4] James doesn't know how to handle this once soft, sensitive, articulate, and secure lady in his life. Now, Sally is anything but.

They have gone from two wages to one. The budget is not only readjusted it's tight, very tight. James is working longer hours to earn that little more. Arguments start, especially when Sally is really emotionally low, over money, job-distribution of tasks around the home, and it seems to James any little topic.

James starts to find things to do in the garage, the shed, and the garden. Going out with the boys, sport and the social club become good escapes. Extra work shifts now don't seem so onerous.

Slowly, emotionally there's a drift. Yet, how do you think Sally feels when James wants to be close again for sex, but then retreats to his 'cave' when things get tense, and her post-natal depressions rolls over her again? How does she feel? Used!

What are they doing? – Developing secondary behaviours, bad secondary behaviours. Their primary behaviour was once their closeness, their intimacy, and their oneness. They both loved their closeness and each other.

Now it's just easier, safer, and emotionally more comfortable for James to keep his distance. After all, "She'll get over it." That's what all the guys at work have said.

"All women go through it. Keep your distance. She'll settle down," offered Bill, James' next-door neighbour. (Yes our dinosaur. Now is Bill really

---

4 http://www.nhmrc.gov.au/_files_nhmrc - Post Natal Depression, Not Just The Baby Blues. Pp. 11.

the source of all wisdom, or truly knows anything about women or relationships? His statement: 'all women go through it' alone is seriously wrong.)

Now let's stop right there.

Research tells us any habit, whether a good one, or a bad one takes from thirty to sixty days to form.[5] So if James is off in 'his shed/his cave' for a couple of months, every time there's a serious difference, and when he's not handling Sally's post-natal depression, over time James will develop a secondary behaviour or a new response that may replace his original positive primary behaviour. Eventually that new behaviour sadly becomes his new primary behaviour or response.

Emotional distance replaces intimacy. "Oh it's just safer," James convinces himself when he has pangs of conviction.

However, on their wedding day didn't they once promise each other: "For better, for worse. In sickness and in heath…"

In his shed one day James thinks long and hard about those words, purposefully uttered on his wedding day. He considers the emotional distance now between them as a couple, and about his inability to understand what Sally was going through medically. Or, more correctly, James ponders on his lack of willingness to want to know about post-natal depression. That frightens him. James knows he doesn't want to end up like Bill next door.

So, James ventures out of his cave and tentatively works his way back into intimacy. James starts to research post-natal depression on the Internet.

"Honey, guess what I've found out the other day," offers James, sipping his coffee, cautiously eyeing Sally. Sally looks up suspiciously. James continues: "I know you're really suffering badly with post-natal depression, and I haven't been much help."

Sally now stops drinking her coffee. Carefully she puts her mug on the glass table next to her and looks directly at James. "Actually, 'any help' may be more like it."

---

5 Cited from various motivational and change agent literature. Statistics reinforced by Phillippa Lally, University College London, in European Journal of Social Psychology, put the average at 66 days.

"You're right honey," James says smiling. "But sweetheart, I apologise. I just didn't know how to respond, having never encountered it before. Absolutely nobody warned us. But, I've found out there are two great clinics in our city that actually specialise in post-natal depression. And if it's all right with you I've made an appointment next week with Dr. Bloomfield for us both. Not for you honey. For us! She's a top specialist in post-natal depression. We're going to tackle this head-on together and win. This is not your problem alone honey. It's ours together."

So united, even if it takes an extended period of time, they confront the issue together with grace, gentleness, and courage. Even when Sally has a bad day and James has a panic attack so everything is screaming, 'run for the cave,' he refuses to run. James holds her. He hugs her. James stands by her. He loves her through the situation.

Maybe sex isn't the highest thing on their agenda at that time. Relationship-building is. And, they're on their way back to intimacy at every level.

James refuses to encourage or develop any relationship-destroying secondary behaviour. He proactively targets their primary behaviour – intimacy. They both allow difficulties – real difficulties – to draw them together, not thrust them apart.

Sally came through her post-natal depression much faster with James supporting her than she ever would have on her own. And, their relationship is not just intact, but deepened because of the crisis. James' initiating concern and a return to none-demanding intimacy and closeness helped Sally most. They retained their primary behaviour. James was caring in his loving behaviours. James was there.

I invite you to consider being aggressively proactive to change. *'Confrontational Change'* is good. Again we emphasise, not confronting our spouse, but confronting yourself. Take change on with the passion of conquering Everest. For this is what great relationships are all about. This is the message of the book.

A 4D Relationship.

We've all seen the incredible 3D images and movies with those special glasses you have to wear. Today, you can purchase a home TV or media unit with 3D capacity. The graphics and action leap out at you in amazing reality.

For a moment, let's put on a really extra special set of glasses of openness and view relationships in amazing 4D, not just 3D.

A great 4D relationship is made up of four important, powerful, positive, and progressive interrelated dimensions. These are:

- **D**esire **D**imension.

- **D**ecision **D**imension.

- **D**emonstration **D**imension.

- **D**etermination **D**imension.

I need to warn however, that there are four very negative 4D's that will try to subversively counterfeit the four positive ones. They will make themselves plain as we move along in the book. When you see the negative attempting to replace the positive honestly ask yourself the question whether indolently you have allowed this destructive attribute to develop in your marriage relationship?

We will develop the positive 4D points more fully in the four Sections to follow that will practically investigate each distinct dimension. However, we need to state that the Fourth Dimension is the catalyst to the other three – either good or bad. Allow me to elaborate.

Over time, I have had friends who have had more 'green thumbs' than they know what to do with. They were brilliant in their garden and glasshouse. They loved the intricacies of gardening and also attempting to develop new varieties of plants. That's not my bag. Though I love my garden and especially keep it neat, I'm afraid all I grow really well in the garden is weeds and tired.

A couple of these individuals come to mind with their ever-consuming quest to find or produce the new or the perfectly original orchid. They spent hours in their glasshouse in painstaking slow procedures attempting to propagate a new species of orchid.

One thing I have noticed was their use of agar (often called agar-agar, a Malay word for local seaweeds). This jelly-like substance, obtained from various seaweeds is used in an absolutely sterile form for bacteriological culture growth, not the least being breeding new plant/orchid strains.

High-grade sterile agar is used extensively in plant biology and development, for a wide variety of plants, and it is often supplemented with essential nutrients and vitamin mixture, suitable to various plants, that allows for seedling germination in petri dishes under absolute sterile conditions. Most often the seeds are produced in a sterile environment.

The Fourth Dimension, this 'Determination' level, includes the catalyst, 'agar' if you like, for each of the other three levels, as well as its own unique qualities. Each of the first three levels will require the reproduction qualities or energy of the Fourth Dimension - determination. But, what is being reproduced in the other three areas?

Sadly if the culture is bad, or not perfectly sterile, it will produce abhorrent, or defective species. Many marriages instead of producing 'The Beauty' are producing 'The Beast.'

It is the choices made, and the 'determination' given to that choice that will produce either a positive or negative in the 'Desire Dimension,' 'Decision Dimension,' and onto the 'Demonstration Dimension.'

Because we deal with this Fourth Dimension last, don't minimise its importance of being fundamental to each of the other three. 'Determination' is the 'glue' of those levels, the foundation substance that will bring life or death to a relationship. The first three dimensions sink their root systems deeply and needfully into the Fourth Dimension. They will draw from what character that dimension has.

When we filter the correct and positive choices with a resolve and 'determination' that causes the marriage to grow, then the 'Desire Dimension' will be positively passionate and the 'Decision Dimension' will be pro-active. Finally, the 'Demonstration Dimension' will follow on and be wonderfully productive.

Consider a graphic presentation below, of the inter-relationship of the three areas of Desire, Decision, and Demonstration with the fourth dimension Determination.

Figure 1
Model Of Effective Marriage

DIMENSION 1 'DESIRE'	DIMENSION 2 'DECISION'	DIMENSION 3 'DEMONSTR-ATION'

DIMENSION 4 'DETERMINATION'

Very briefly the four dimensions are:

Firstly, Desire: There must be an intense 'desire' to the relationship, embracing the purity of that desire, passion, and other exciting things. This is the *motivational side* of the relationship, and it allows us to see how important maintaining passion is to any successful relationship. Desires are influenced by the choices and 'determination' of the Fourth Dimension.

Secondly, Decision: A committed 'decision' side to the relationship must exist and be constantly worked on. Through life's difficulties and hiccups, resolve will see you through. This decision process is the *mental ascent or cognitive decision side* of the commitment, influenced by our choices and 'determination' to follow them through.

Thirdly, Demonstration: 'Demonstration' of the relationship must not only be entered into, but also 'seen to be' entered into. Here, the *emotional side of the relationship* finds itself worked out in deepening intimacy. In this area, we demonstrate daily the loving relationship in positive ways in the little as well as the big things of life that we do for each other. Again, our choices will be evidenced by our 'determination.'

Fourthly, Determination: There will be a 'determination' side to the relationship that will influence the other three dimensions. We trust that influence will be positive. Positive, pro-marriage choices are made with an open consciousness of our destiny. The destiny side of our relationship is fulfilled by ***powerful positive choices***. These choices and the determination given to them will affect a positive or negative response in the first three dimensions.

Some may interpret this 'Determination' aspect of the marriage as 'commitment.' I'm fine with that. I made a vow to my wife, Pauline, at our wedding many years ago and I'm 'committed to keeping it,' no matter what. That's determination. Determination is commitment. Some would even go one step further and say that is 'covenant.'

To illustrate these four progressive and life-injecting forces in a healthy marriage relationship we will be challenging many of the old verbal sayings and adages about life, and relationships, which have become layered in our subconscious – eg: 'It is better to give than receive.' What absolute nonsense if you blindly apply this axiom in isolation to any healthy growing relationship. If in the relationship all you ever do is give, and never ever receive, you will ultimately be deeply disappointed, feel used and disillusioned in that relationship.

So we must confront life to maintain an enriching marriage. This very principle of healthy confrontation, which we suggest as being part of the core philosophy of this book, is what we will apply to the development process of a healthy marriage.

Were the old sayings, oft quoted, always correct? No, not always! Now, I understand there is a measure of truth in each of the old expressions, and they were trying to illustrate a point, but they are not all that helpful if applied in their totality or simplicity – especially today. What attitudes are the old sayings conveying?

An Examination Of Older, Some Out-dated Attitudes:

First The Negative

I remember a sad case in point. A little bubbly 3-year-old girl, pretty as a picture with golden curls to her shoulders and full of life, asks the obvious question to any three-year old, about a heavily pregnant lady in the shopping mall.

"Mummy, why does that lady have a big tummy?"

Normally that wouldn't have fazed 'mummy,' but today there was a potential problem. Nana, (prim and proper Nana), the little girl's great-grandmother, is along for the shopping trip.

With gasps of unbelievable disbelief Nana decrees: "Shush child. Carol can't you do something about her. She's embarrassing all of us."

No, actually only Nana is embarrassed. And that's her problem – no one else. Sadly, great-grandma tries to impose her view as everybody else's. The gorgeous three-year old is not satisfied with Nana's 'shush.' Her mother tries to explain that the lady has a baby in her stomach. Nana turns her head and tries to show she's deliberately not listening to such scandalous talk, but goes ever increasing shades of red, as she specifically and deliberately takes in every word, even edging ever so slowly closer to better listen.

Nana firmly holds to the old adage and tenant: *'Children should be seen and not heard.'* What utter garbage in its absolute enforcement. We're not here talking about a precocious, loudmouth, and arrogantly rude child. We're simply talking about an honest reasonable enquiry from a three-year old. Nana's generation sadly and rarely communicated life skills and life truths, definitely little about sex.

Let's seriously challenge Nana and her out-dated expression, because today countless hundreds of thousand of children are 'not being heard' as they sadly fall victim to sexual predators. We want to and need to create a healthy family environment and community culture where children will lovingly be both seen and lovingly heard.

So we will challenge old, sometimes useless sayings.

You can guess what the next question of our gorgeous bubbly three-year old is.

"Well Mummy, how did the baby get in there and how does the baby get out?"

These are obvious questions for an innocent, non-offensive three-year old. But, not for Nana. She's already almost fainted on the spot. Great-grandma has to sit down at such licentious talk. And, if Nana hadn't already had her hair permed with a soft shade of purple what her gorgeous great-grandchild has just asked will quickly curl her hair.

Interestingly, Nana has already this morning severely criticised a teenager at the mall for having bright red hair, gelled into spikes. But of course her purple hair is perfectly acceptable. Some people have strange rationale, don't they?

Very astutely a pretty, cute little three-year old, who will become a wondrous teenager, quickly and clearly picks up as she grows up: "Nana thinks that sex is dirty."

We need to confront such nonsense. So, the point of this book is to help you confront. Confront whom? Confront your spouse? No! Confront yourself, attitudes and your thinking. For in positively confronting yourself we will mature in wisdom and practise.

Now The Positive

Thomas Carlyle once said: *'Endurance is patience concentrated.'* Now there's a positive adage if you ever heard one. Great athletes and noted leaders have lived endurance into fame.

On the 16th July 2003[6] the darling of Australian women track and field events, Cathy Freeman, officially retired. She was a superstar of international fame and rapport. We understand all athletes must reach a point when retirement is necessary, but listen to her words in her July 16th interview, as to why Cathy was retiring:

"I've lost that want, that drive, that passion."

Cathy retired a hero. Her endurance was waning. Another interview at that time showed her saying:

"I can't say I'd feel that sense of fulfilment again."

---

6 Cited from various Australian newspapers of July 17th, 2003.

Do you at times feel like retiring from your marriage? Could it be that you can lose your 'want,' your 'drive' and 'passion?' Without these vital ingredients your relationship will flounder. Have you seemingly lost your sense of fulfilment and endurance?

As Cathy Freeman knew, drive, passion and a consuming sense of fulfilment were necessary to be an enduring winner on the track. So it is in marriage.

Consider challenging the need of drive, passion and fulfilment, thoroughly reactivating their presence in your relationship. They are continually necessary and vital components.

Why can't we think about marriage emulating physics in clear discernable, workable laws?

Isaac Newton's Laws Of Motion, Or Was It Relationship?

Isaac Newton stands as a giant in the annals of history with his Laws of Motion and work in physics and mathematics. Ask yourself was he really talking *only* about motion, mere physics, or mathematics? The opening chapter in each Section of the book has a serialised fictitious continuing story woven around our mathematical and physics genius, Isaac Newton.

I have 'light-heartedly' theorised Isaac really was also commenting about human relationships, not just physics alone, but because of the sensibilities of his time disguised his thoughts, concerning relational and marriage harmony, as ideas about motion. No matter what you think, surely as you look at his three laws they do have an interesting application towards everyday relationships, especially marriage and family harmony.

With just a little twist of history, but remaining totally true to every historical fact (and we here plead forgiveness from the purists of history), we create a scenario and setting for this work that is at least worthy of consideration, for the sheer fun of it.

Trust you enjoy the insights into Isaac Newton and some of his friends. May his three Laws of Motion/Relationship, and a fourth law of physics, speak into every one of our relationships for the challenge they can present to all of us.

Section 1

Desire, Passion, And Other Exciting Things.

What incredible energy courting couples demonstrate. If you could only harness this consuming force, you could run a power station off it. What motivates them? Desire! Passionate, wondrous desire! If the relationship loses it, the couple usually quickly lose interest in each other.

For many happy couples this desire remains a key feature throughout their marriage, though it may be transformed into a myriad of unique and varying manifestations. Tragically for some desire lasts only for a short time after marriage, then sadly dissipates away. If, as Wood and Nimkoff state, as earlier cited, up to 80% of romantic love potentially diminishes in the average marriage in the first two years, then every couple needs to passionately (no pun intended), and actively work on retaining the 'desire' aspect of their relationship.

Why does that passion subside for some couples? Why can't that motivation continue throughout the relationship? It can. It's just that we have to make a conscious decision to keep desire and love alive. What can we do to keep the life-giving spark and love alive?

You need to constantly confront your attitudes. Don't settle for rest and inertia. Keep the relationship alive and moving, not subdued and taken over by lazy attitudes. Keep momentum and refuse to be knocked off course.

There has to be a deliberate personal and couple's 'determination' to make well-intended decisions about positive choices that will produce life, not death in our relationship.

One

Isaac Newton And His Apple.

Isaac Newton sat under his favourite fruit-bearing apple tree looking out over the quiet rolling green hills, grain-filled fields, and brown, dusty ploughed paddocks of Cambridge. This hilltop, with a lone large apple tree, overlooking a stream was Isaac's secret hideaway from all the maddening demands and oft-intellectual snobbery of Trinity College. Isaac was a fellow of Trinity College and the second Lucasian Professor of Mathematics at the University of Cambridge. This was then one of the most prestigious academic posts in the then known world.

In the distance Isaac could see a young couple in a field playfully chasing each other around a haystack, oblivious that anybody could see them. Round and round they went, often accidentally on purpose falling into each other's arms, then off they would run again. They then settled to sit on the banks of the stream, his arm around her, with her head on his shoulder.

"What would they be saying to each other? Sweet words of love no doubt. How odd!" Isaac mused. "How odd! Yet, how wonderful." This wasn't a cynical comment from Isaac, but the thoughtful reflection of a single man, concerning and comparing the many marriages he constantly saw around him at Cambridge University and in everyday life.

Isaac Newton lay back on the soft green grass thinking of what he had just seen. It didn't match up at all with most of the couples he knew. What about John his friend, a fellow-professor at Trinity, and his wife Mary? What a dull couple they were. Hardly had Isaac ever heard or seen a gentle or endearing, let alone a romantic word or action from either of them towards each other.

Then there was Edward and Elizabeth who had developed an almost sadistic cutting cynicism with each other in private, but acted anything but in public. What a great example of a hypocritical marriage they were.

"Hypocrites," Isaac said out loud, whilst thinking about the contrasts of the two couples he knew and the young couple he had just seen in the field. After hearing giggling in the distance Isaac sat up and looked again for his mystery duo once sitting by the stream. They were now walking hand in hand unaware of their silent observer.

"But, what would I know about relationships?" Isaac muttered. He thought about his own single life and close, endearing relationships.

On Christmas Day 1642 in the Manor of Woolsthorpe in Lincolnshire, Isaac Newton came screaming into this world as a premature baby. Shouldn't it have been a joyous occasion for a couple? However, it was not to be. Isaac's father had died of a sudden illness three months before he was born. Isaac had been named after his deceased father. Had that soul-wrenching loss of her husband brought such grief and pain to his mother that she delivered Isaac early? Who knows?

Isaac thought for a moment. "What was it they said of my father? Oh yes, 'a wild, extravagant and weak yeoman farmer.' Maybe it's better I didn't know him."

'At least Isaac had a mother to love him,' you might say. Not quite. Hannah, Isaac's mother, left him to live with his maternal grandmother when he was only three years of age, as she had remarried. A sixty-three-year old rector of North Witham, a Barnabas Smith by name, became Isaac's absentee step-dad.

"Blasted vicar," Isaac muttered.

It could never be said that Isaac Newton had the fairest of deals, when it came to parents or role models for healthy relationships. He eventually never married. Was Isaac affected by his mother's remarriage and abandonment? We can only surmise.

"Why is it that the couples I know are so inert, so dead in their re-lationship? Yet, this couple," Isaac muttered, staring at the young lovers in the meadow walking back to the village obviously deeply in love, "are abounding in energy, life, action, and fun? Elizabeth and Edward, John, and Mary represent everything that's average, stale, mundane, and lifeless about a relationship. However, these two," Isaac thought, as he stared with a new fascination after the couple now climbing a country stile, "are full of life. They make things happen." The young man caught his beloved as she playfully pretended to fall off the stile. Isaac stood staring at them.

"That's it," Isaac said out loud. "They 'make' things happen."

Isaac lay down again on the soft green grass. Then, something hit him. What, revelation, a great thought? No a ripe apple!

"What the..." Isaac yelled as he sat up clutching his head with the offend-ing apple falling into his lap. In that one historic moment that apple became possibly the second most infamous piece of fruit, second only to Adam and Eve's. This was now the second time this apple invading, mind expanding, brain-banging experience had occurred to Isaac.

When only 23 years old Isaac had been forced to leave his beloved Cambridge because of the threat of a plague. Back home at Woolsthorpe Manor, safe from the plague he watched an apple fall and began to ponder on physics principles. Now, the concept was 'hitting' him all over again.

In 1666 whilst at Woolsthorpe Isaac thought through and formulated the basis of his three Laws of Motion, though he did not publish his work till 1687. 1666 became known to Isaac as *Annus Mirabillis* or better under-stood as 'Miracle Year.' His genius was beginning to unfold and confront the world.

"Stupid apple," Isaac said, as he was about to throw it away. But, he stopped. Staring at the apple in his hand Isaac's mind was alive at the implica-tions of his laws. He stared after the couple now a faint speck in the distance, heading towards the village near the manor.

Isaac's thoughts raced. "I was at rest, and one apple brought me to action. Most of my friend's relationships are at rest; no I think almost dead. Yet, the couple I've seen today is full of life, not at rest at all."

Laws of relationship started to cram his thinking. However, this was the early 1680's and you didn't speak about relationships, marriage and especially marital intimacy, not openly. No way. No one dared. How could Isaac hide such truths? "I know," he smiled, "I'll just extend thinking about my laws of motion. Explain the principle as if it's physics, not relationship." Isaac chuckled, as he thought about it further.

Thinking of Elizabeth and Edward along with John and Mary it was clear that a relationship at rest remains at rest. "Dead, lazy. That's what they are. Yet, that couple by the haystack, they have motion and are moving at an exciting pace in their relationship. Only something hitting them off-course, like has happened to Elizabeth and Edward, with his adultery, will affect or stop their desire for each other," Isaac thought.

"How can I express the idea best?"

Isaac spent time trying to formulate ideas that would be socially acceptable. He couldn't come right out and speak about relationships. What would the 'easily offended gentry' think of that?

"Who cares?" Isaac pondered for a minute. Then, an idea struck him, just as quickly as the offending apple that had crowned him a short while ago.

"Ahh, I have it. Hiding my rules of relationship in my rules of motion will provide the camouflage necessary. I'll call a relationship a body, in motion or otherwise. No one will know the difference. Now how can I cleverly disguise it?" Isaac stood, walked and talked to himself.

*"**A body** [marriage/relationship] **at rest remains at rest**, yet a **body** [marriage/relationship] **in motion continues to move at a constant speed along a straight line, unless in either case, the body** [the marriage] **is acted upon by an outside force.**"* [Laws Of Motion No. 1]

Isaac could sense that the couple he had seen, now vanished from sight, were in motion. They were headed in a clear direction. Driven by desire, passion, and fun they were making their relationship work. That was the key – Desire!

His various friends had settled for their relationship at rest, in fact, dead in the water. What had stopped them? What had knocked them off course? Work, careers, social acceptance and a dozen other demands had all contributed to become outside forces that stopped their meaningful marriage relationship dead in its tracks. Then neglecting their marriage had opened them up to destructive behaviours that tried to fill the void, like Edward's adulterous affairs.

Thinking of the couple Isaac had observed he further pondered: "Will this young couple also lose their momentum? Possibly. But, why can't this couple keep their passion, illustrated by the incredible desire they have for each other now? Why can't they be alive permanently in their marriage?" mused Isaac as he wandered back to Trinity College.

The Challenge: *Is your marriage still alive, passionate, moving and full of fun? Can you feel the passionate 'desire' still active within the relationship, no matter how long married? Or, has the marriage come to rest, and been knocked off course by some outside force?*

Two

The Honeymoon Won't Last Forever.

Chris and Clyde were in their mid thirties and had been married for several years. As yet no children had arrived. Deep down Chris was having reservation about their relationship. Chris wanted children, but she was more than concerned about what their marriage had turned into. Not that she didn't love Clyde, but where was the fun they used to have? He was now always so serious.

One research study[7] showed that women report that for them the two biggest causes of a relationship becoming stale are 'routine,' and 'boredom.' Chris knew all about this. She was getting bored in the relationship, really bored with what she called her: 'boring routine'!

Normally Nigel's flirting at work would have been brushed off and ignored with the disgust, contempt, and rejection such actions deserved. Now Nigel's constant flirting worried her that it stroked her 'emotional feathers,' and ego in ways Chris knew only Clyde should influence her. But, it had been so long since he had even bothered.

Arguments at home were becoming more frequent and intense between them. Nigel was sounding more attractive by the week. It seemed to Clyde

---

7 Boredom Kills Marriage. Elena Gorgan. Pub: GMT. April 2009. Also confirmed by Elizabeth Scott in her 2011 study: Maintaining A Happy Marriage.

that he only agreed to a weekend away out of a pressured desperation from Chris. Eventually, they both decided on a long weekend at a mountain retreat, away from the perceived pressures and expectations of home.

It had been a very pleasant three-day break for both of them. They went for long walks along the mountain paths surrounded by soft dark green moss and grey-green lichen covered boulders with gentle fragrant alpine flowers and heathers of brilliant colour and subdued earthy tones, braving patches of snow. The tall dark-green pines smelled so beautiful, clean and fresh. Pinecones lay in the snow scattered like Christmas decorations.

The sun was slowly setting on their second day away; as they skipped rocks across the sun-glinting surface of a smooth perfectly still alpine lake, reflecting a deep jade green colour. Not even a breeze caused a ripple. They climbed further up the hillside and sat on a rough-sawn log seat, surrounded by thick patches of snow, with a fresh flowering soft lilac-coloured crocus just breaking through the snow. The seat half way up the mountain looked down at the long finger-shaped lake, adjacent to the lodge. The lodge, made from natural stone and rough-sawn logs, stood out in the clearing. Smoke lazily rose from the all-natural stone chimney. The whole scene was tranquillity personified.

Chris expressed her inner thoughts.

"Honey, this has been wonderful. It's almost as if we were just married again." Chris almost sighed the words as she laid her head on Clyde's shoulder. She felt distinctively Clyde's body immediately and suddenly tighten, and Chris sat up as he spoke.

"What are you implying? Aren't you happy with our marriage now?" Chris was shocked at Clyde's unexpected angry retort.

From that point onwards the conversation seemed to degenerate into recriminatory comments from both sides. "What has happened to the romance and passion in our lives?" Chris pleaded, sobbing through tears.

"Everybody knows that the 'honeymoon won't last forever.' Who do you know that has kept honeymoon love alive?" demanded Clyde.

'Everybody?' Did he really mean 'everybody?' Well that wasn't quite true. However, nobody had bothered to tell Clyde that. Chris still felt strongly that the passion, joy, desire and romance of the honeymoon should continue for a couple. "Why should romance and desire end?" Chris pleaded, "Why?"

Clyde looked on helpless. He had no easy answer. After all wasn't the marital experience Clyde saw in his own mother and father's relationship a lifeless, passionless, almost aggressive marriage? Chris on the other hand was immersed in a fanciful world of Mills & Boon, and she more and more marginalised her expectations in marriage to the seducing world of romance literature and TV soaps. For Chris this had merely been an escape.

Clyde had often stopped to see what Chris was reading. "Ah, ha!" he said on one occasion, *"Lord Bedworth's Truest Love."* Clyde turned the book over to read the back cover. "Well, here we have it. 'A blonde, broken-hearted, sultry heroine changes the course of destiny and history.' Yet there's more. 'Lord Bedworth, wounded by life, withdrawn, member of nobility has his passions awakened...' But wait," said Clyde with that note of sarcasm in his voice, theatrically playing to a hostile audience. "There's even more. 'She, his passionate soul mate, he the handsome dashing Lord' Oh for goodness sake! What utter garbage." Clyde had thrown the book onto the lounge at Chris' feet, as he walked away. Chris had felt crushed.

Now today, there was more than a chill in the late afternoon, early evening air from the snowbound mountain peaks. However, they both persisted and battled through to hear each other. They listened, really listened to each other for the first time in ages. As painful as some points were they determined together to bring the passion, the desire, and the romance back into their relationship.

As they walked back to their mountain resort purposefully hand in hand, as a deliberate gesture of commitment, they knew they had to work on their marriage, and together made a decision to return to the intensity of their courting days and early marriage. The lodge below them was ablaze with lights. The path around them got darker by the minute. It seemed to symbolise their personal journey as they walked out of the dark towards the light.

The coming weeks brought a freshness, spontaneity, and passion that thrilled both of them. Their desire was being rekindled slowly but surely.

Clyde was sure Chris was far more responsive to him sexually. Chris loved the return of her former lover – Clyde. Nigel – well he went to flirt with someone else, as he wasn't making any more headway with Chris.

Keeping passion and desire alive in a relationship are vital. Their continued presence doesn't allow an emotional and empathic vacuum to develop that can be filled by another person. Don't let familiarity breed contempt.

I tell people that Pauline and I have a very platonic relationship. They look aghast. "Oh, yes it's platonic all right. We like to play, and it's a tonic!" Need one say more?

I fully understand that as married couples, in living together, we may start to take each other for granted, if we let such happen. That is where we need to become confrontational. I need to confront issues – not Pauline. Why? Doesn't Pauline need to be passionate, romantic, and have desire for the relationship? Absolutely! However, our primary concept in this book is not specifically about what changes a spouse can or should make, but what changes we personally can and must make.

If I understand that the top two stalers in a relationship for a woman is often cited as boredom and routine, then what am I doing to change that? I must confront 'me,' not Pauline. Don't let the relationship stall. Don't presume he or she is still chasing.

In the tragic aftermath of a marriage breakdown through adultery, an abandoned wife said. "Oh, I knew he wasn't as passionate as he used to be, but I presumed he was still chasing me. The trouble was he was chasing someone else, and I was too dumb and busy in my own world to realise it. I knew she was chasing him. I just presumed he was running away, and I did nothing to help him run after me."

When your car stalls in the railway crossing, you're a sitting duck to get hit by the train. Keep the relationship moving with passion and romance. I don't think I need to really define what they are, do I?

In a poll taken a few years ago 76% of the newly married couples responding indicated and named 'love' as the major reason for marrying. Interestingly ten years later when a psychologist asked 75,000 wives, married for some time, to evaluate the reason they would originally have chosen to wed 'love' was by far still the most important issue. Well if love holds such an important place in our minds as well as our hearts over time why don't we work just as hard at staying married as we did at getting married?

A young man, nervous about his impending wedding was having an afternoon coffee with Allan, his future brother-in-law.

"Congratulations," said Allan. "I'm sure you will look back at today and remember this as the happiest day of your life." Greg, the nervous groom looked up.

"But, I'm not getting married till tomorrow," protested Greg.

"I know," replied Allan. "That's exactly what I mean."

And that, sad to say, is how many people negatively view marriage. So many assume that it's almost acceptable to sling off at marriage and joke at its expense. Funny, isn't it, that you rarely hear jokes about violent arguments or abuse – how funny they are? The reality is they destroy a relationship.

'The Honeymoon Won't Last Forever.' Who said? Obviously that applies to someone who isn't interested in keeping his or her relationship alive.

Pauline and I are not particularly keen on certain well-worn rhetoric or sayings, such as: 'falling in love.' If you think about the expression for a while it sounds like a terrible accident. We prefer the term 'rising in love.' From the point when a couple meet and commit to each other there should be a gentle and continual rising in love, not a falling – before and after marriage.

Being 'perfect' puts such pressure on the relationship. It's the stuff of fights. Sure you can find the 'perfect' character in a TV soapie, or romance novel (well I know that stretches the imagination). But, life is filled with challenges they don't seem to face or understand.

Keep passion, romance, and spontaneous joy alive in your relationship. May desire just for each other, be an important driving force in our marriage.

Three

PRACTICE MAKES PERFECT.

Do you really think we ever get to a state of being 'perfect'? It seems the better that we get at something the more someone moves the goal posts. As we continue to keep passion, desire and fun alive in the relationship we reach a stage where changes occur. Two becomes three, four, and maybe five. Ah yes, then there's inheriting the mortgage.

Will we become perfect? No, I think we should aim at becoming flexible. What was 'perfect' when we were in our twenties maybe doesn't quite cut it when we're in our forties. When we have inherited two children, a dog, a cat, and a mortgage life changes.

Flexibility is essential. Aim to enjoy life, not become perfect. Oh, you think you're the ultimate lover in your thirties? Hang around a while and see what challenges come to your body in your sixties and seventies.

Perfection is not what we should be seeking; it is flexibility – joyful flexibility. Doesn't perfection bring such demands? Flexibility is relaxing. Lighten up, learn to embrace joyful interaction with life and those essential others in your life.

Keeping a sense of humour about yourself is so important. I take my marriage very seriously. However, I try not to take myself too seriously. Learn to laugh at yourself. We all make mistakes. When the 'perfect' rather than the 'flexible' complex possesses us we will fail ourselves as well as our relationship.

The perfect partner may exist in a romance novel. Tragically they rarely reflect real life. Being flexible with each other is far more real and relaxing.

Did we let mistakes put us off when we were courting? Absolutely not! When something went wrong, we often apologised, had a good laugh, and got on with life. Why change a winning formula?

Keep trying to be better in every skill of relationship-building. Is it really perfection we are after? If perfection drives you then you will put enormous pressure on yourself, your spouse and your relationship. Marriage is a growing, developing skill. Maybe we will never arrive at perfection. We should be just content to enjoy the journey.

Research has shown that couples who can learn to 'laugh with each other,' instead of 'at each other,' evidence a far more relaxed relationship. Nobody likes being laughed at. It humiliates, it debases.

However, when we can laugh at ourselves laughing keeps the passion alive. Remember, we did a lot of laughing in our courting days. One interesting illustration from the United States showed that different states of mind, and attitudes to fun and laughter, when one rides a roller coaster, have directly opposite physiological effects upon the body.

If you love roller coasters and throughout the entire ride are yelling and laughing out loud, hands in the air with excitement, thrill, exhilaration and fun, then your body has been thoroughly conditioned for health. Oxygen has coursed through your system in pressured amounts doing you good. Hormonal secretions, interleukin[8] and interferons[9] that assist in preventing cancer and boosting a positive immune system have been abundantly released into your bloodstream.

---

8 It has been found that interleukins are produced by a wide variety of body cells. The function of the immune system depends in a large part on *interleukins*, and rare deficiencies of a number of them have been described, all featuring autoimmune diseases or immune deficiency.

9 Interferons are proteins made and released by host cells in response to the presence of pathogens such as viruses, bacteria, parasites, even tumour cells. They allow for communication between cells to trigger the protective defences of the immune system that eradicate pathogens or tumours/cancer.

One medical comment showed that if you tragically have cancer and were to have a full course of injections over time of these life-giving secretions to combat the disease, in Australia such could cost well over $100,000. Yet one joyful, fun-filled ride on a roller coaster could produce (not that it could be harvested), up to $1,000,000 worth of these life-generating agencies.

No wonder the ancient proverb says: 'Laughter doeth good like a medicine.'

However, if you hate roller coasters, and your ride finds you with clenched teeth, tightened shoulders, and eyes jammed shut for the whole ride, can anyone suggest you have had a health-injecting experience? No. Now, no longer are healthy secretions interleukin/interferons released but excessive and unhealthy amounts of cortisone and adrenalin. They surge in your system in toxic amounts. Now those massive over-abundant secretions in that one roller coaster ride are harmful, being excessively greater than the balanced normal demands. They can drastically decrease the effectiveness of your overall immune system.

It's interesting how two entirely different states of mind can produce two entirely different physiological responses from exactly the same event. One brings life. The other can seriously deplete the immune system and well being of the body.

So don't aim at perfection. Get passionate about improvement and flexibility. Learn to laugh at yourself. Do the body good. Keep trying to be and do better. Never give up.

Norman Cousins was diagnosed with a very serious life-threatening illness. His long-term life forecast was grim. Quality of life was very poor. There was very little they could do for him but make him more comfortable. Determined to enjoy his remaining months and weeks Norman hired all the funniest movies he could find, and decided to enjoy life having a good laugh. He also read the classics in humorous books.

Cousins recounted his own self-treatment with humour in an article in the New England Journal of Medicine in 1976, after he'd been diagnosed with a very painful, life-threatening form of arthritis called ankylosing spondylitis. Doctors gave him little chance of recovery. When traditional medicine failed to relieve his pain, Cousins left the hospital, checked into a hotel for a month, took mega-doses of vitamin C and watched Marx Brothers and Laurel & Hardy films alongside TV sitcom funny comedies, finding that 10 minutes of 'belly laughter' allowed him two hours of pain-free sleep. He eventually recovered and wrote a series of best-selling books on humour and healing.

He did nothing but laugh and laugh each day for one whole month. He also wrote original jokes, which he would read aloud to himself then laugh like crazy. He noticed that every time he laughed, his pain was eased. At the end of one month, Cousins returned to the hospital for a check-up. To the surprise of the medical staff that examined him, they found no trace of the dreaded disease. He was completely cured! Cousins had been diagnosed in the mid 1960s, and earlier had been told by doctors that they could do little for him. He lived till 1990.

The doctors and hospital asked Cousins what medicines he took that cured him. They would not believe him when he replied he had not taken any medicine since he was told his ailment was incurable. The medical specialists insisted: "You must have done something you never did before." He finally replied: "All I did was to laugh myself to health." Later Cousins was even appointed a faculty member of the University of California Los Angeles School of Medicine, although he was not a doctor.

In his well-respected book: *'Anatomy Of An Illness,'* [10] Cousins documents scientifically how that he laughed his way to health. His book is highly respected in medical circles, and his recovery from illness is authenticated at a medical professional level. It's well worth a read.

Listen to some of his interesting statements: *"Drugs are not always necessary [but] belief in recovery always is."* And also: *"... detailed the negative effects of the negative emotions on body chemistry."* Finally: *"I made the joyous discovery that ten minutes of genuine belly laughter had an anaesthetic effect and would give me at least two hours of pain-free sleep."* Norman Cousins knew how to laugh, and 'it did him good.'

Maybe we should keep trying, laughing at our mistakes and learning to lighten up, rather than trying to be perfect.

---

10   Anatomy Of An Illness. Norman Cousins. Pub: W. W. Norton Company. Original press 1979. Several reprints since.

Sadly Tony and Cheryl, both forty-five years old, seem to have given up on their marriage. Once a happy, fun-filled duo, they now have degenerated into such a serious couple. Two children had made it through to adult life, not impressed with either Mum or Dad.

"Lighten up Dad. You're too serious. You never laugh and enjoy life any more. Boy you're dull." Their son David's response was in return to his Dad's verbal tirade about him improperly mowing the lawn. David, in trying to help his Dad out, had mowed the lawn his way. In mowing he had mowed his name in huge letters on the back lawn.

Both David and his sister Samantha were pleased to live on their respective university campuses. Life growing up in a home where perfection was demanded seemed so exacting.

Counselling hadn't helped Tony or Cheryl. The counsellor pointed out that they didn't seem to have any fun in their marriage. This had brought a quick caustic response from Tony.

"Good grief man. Get real. What, do you think we're running? A circus?" Tony had become the ultimate successful serious businessman.

Tony was aware that Cheryl was about to walk. Not a word had been said, but there were just those subtle indicators. Nothing brought the crisis home to him better than his Friday night work staff Christmas party.

Tony had such fun. Laughing, joking and interacting with the other staff members he was the life of the party. Jacob, the Sales Manager only said a few words, but they were uncomfortable: "Tony, you're such fun to be around."

Those words froze in Tony's mind. They were the complete and exact opposite to Cheryl's words spoken that very same morning as Tony, angry with Cheryl, over virtually nothing, left for the office. "Tony, you're no fun to be around. What has happened to you – to us?"

As Tony drove back home from the party he did some serious soul-searching. He pulled off the busy highway, a few kilometres from home at a local pub. Tony didn't need a drink. He just needed to sit in the car park and think.

"Cheryl's right," Tony thought. "Why is it I can have fun at work, but not at home?" Tony was confronting himself. He made some decisions that night sitting alone in a hotel car park. Switching the engine on he pulled out into the traffic determined to make some real changes.

As Tony came through the door he yelled up the stairs: "Hey, Cheryl, put your glad rags on we're going out." Despite her protests, as she was already in her nightwear, he made her change.

They painted the town red dancing and partying till nearly 2.00am Saturday morning at a pre-Christmas function put on by one of their city's large hotels, which was a client of the company where Tony worked.

Cheryl couldn't believe the change in him as Tony joked and laughed all night.

It must have been over three years since Tony had done anything this spontaneous. Cheryl tightly snuggled against him that night in an intimate spooning position as they both drifted off to sleep exhausted. They had made love that night. No, I don't mean sex. They had created, 'made,' produced, given love to each other in sharing the joy of fun, laughter, and spontaneity.

Cheryl couldn't believe her breakfast in bed later that morning, with a white rose from her garden on the side of the tray. A soft moist tear formed.

They say it takes up to three to five kilometres to turn a huge oil tanker around when at sea, with a turning circle of up to three kilometres.

No, everything wasn't totally turned around for Tony and Cheryl in that one event. However, they both knew the boat had begun to slowly turn.

It is not perfection we should be seeking, its flexibility. Learn to roll with the punches, enjoy life, laugh a little or a lot – just laugh. It's good for the body. Be passionate about life.

I have noticed that those who are passionate about life are often passionate about each other and enjoy good humour. Therefore stir up the fun-based, pressure-free expectations to be ourselves that we had as courting couples.

Laugh at your mistakes. Promise yourself you will do better next time, and then get on with life.

Thinking about laughing at your mistakes, have you heard about the woman who was married four times – once to a multi-millionaire, then to an actor, then to a minister, and finally to an undertaker. Which only proves: One for the money, two for the show, three to get ready and four to go.

Four

ABSENCE MAKES THE HEART GROW FONDER.

Pauline and I travel a lot in our speaking engagements around the world. Sometimes I make these trips alone. So, I know the power of absence making the heart grow fonder. I really admire the sacrifice of those early explorers that were away from their wife and family sometimes for years. I don't know how they did it. Today, even though we are apart there is email, incredible Skype, phones, near out-dated faxes and wonderful 'Inter-flora.'

When i'm away alone i choose different ways to express my love. I specifically and deliberately choose to be proactive to keep the desire in our relationship on 'active.' Distance can enhance a relationship.

I remember when pauline and i were engaged her mother, in all her draconian wisdom decided: "ivan you can only come over three nights a week. Do you understand? Three nights a week!"

It felt like my throat was cut. I wanted to spend as much time with pauline as possible. Then, a thought struck me: "she said nothing about the weekends; she only said week, meaning week-days." So i was deliberately going over to pauline's three nights monday to friday and then also arriving saturday and sunday. Then to spice up the arrangements pauline would come over occasionally to my place on other nights. Well, that's not me going over there, now is it?

My mother-in-law took three months to wake up to my little scheme. I knew i wanted to spend as much time with pauline as possible. I still do.

Ted and beverly don't enjoy quality time together. They enjoy their own lifestyles. Their 'own space' is what they call it. This phrase today in our society is so often tragically over-used in a self-centred and self-ish way. Though they have been together for six and a half years and in their mid twenties, ted and beverly lead pretty separate lives. That deep passion and desire for togetherness has slipped out of their relationship long ago.

No one could suggest that they don't enjoy sex when they get together, but their sex-life seems more based on what they get, rather than what they give, being totally self-absorbed. This is not a healthy trait. Selfish self-centredness drives them both.

When they clash, ted goes down to the shed to immerse himself in his hobby – boat building. What is it with some guys and their cave? It seems to ted that he's down in the shed most of his spare time. Sadly 'disinterest' is replacing 'desire.'

Absence doesn't always make their hearts grow fonder. Ted and beverly are using absence as a way of avoiding each other. Just waiting for each other to cool down before coexisting in the same house again is no way to keep passion and desire alive.

Sure ted has a desire for sex, but has lost loving as a habit for beverly. They need to, but cannot, meet each other's needs in every area of life, not just in the bedroom.

Beverly's shifts, as an airhostess take her regularly away from home. But, she is now gradually finding her overseas stay-overs very welcome relief from home. Ted is sure that beverly is actively and deliberately applying for the overseas shifts and trips.

Ted and beverly won't confront the problem. They avoid it. Both come from homes where their parents were classic 'avoiders.' Worst still they think this is acceptable, even the norm.

They are not keeping their desire and passion for each other alive whilst at home. The presence of passion and desire expressed only in the bedroom worries beverly. She wants a man who is passionate about her in every area of their marriage. "What was i thinking, marrying so young?"

Pregnant just after her nineteenth birthday to ted, beverly felt intense pressure from both families to marry. "What will the neighbours think?" Was the selfish and uncaring cry of a hysterical father. So they married when beverly was three months pregnant. Then, beverly and ted tragically lost their baby at six months in a car crash. Beverly felt trapped in a relationship forced on her. Sure ted had passionately loved her. But, where was that desire, that passion now?

Her parents weren't any help about the loss of their child. "Maybe its for the best dear." Beverly and ted suffered with no support.

Ted couldn't come to terms with the accident and the loss of their child, though the accident was not his fault. Youth, inexperience, and bad role modelling from parents caused them both to close down, instead of opening up to each other. They never thought about counselling.

Absences didn't make their hearts grow fonder. They needed help to relieve the pain. They really needed to rediscover the joy of the investment of time with each other for the joy of being together. Nearness to build intimacy, not sex, was tragically missing.

As you may know marriage is like a violin. After the music stops, the strings are still attached. Who says the music has to stop? Some other cynic has said marriage is like a midnight phone call. You get a ring, and then you wake up. Though i'll use these humorous quips ask yourself what it really says about society's view of marriage?

Some years ago psychology today magazine did some interesting research on why couples stay together.[11] What was the key 'staying factor' in a healthy and happy relationship? The number one answer they discovered was: 'time spent together.'

Now i want you to extend your thinking. Do you only interpret 'time spent together' as physical time when physically together? Right now, as i type this chapter i am in exeter in the united kingdom, conducting a community

---

11 Psychology Today, 1986. Further developed in: Till Death Do Us Part: How Couples Stay Together. Jeanette & Robert Laurer. Pub: Hayworth Press. 1986.

marriage/relationship seminar. I have already this morning emailed pauline, who is not on this trip, with general chitchat as well as a little love poem i made up just for her. We will chat tonight on the phone. I have also communicated back to my office (as they know exactly what i want) to arrange flowers to go to pauline in a few days time.

Now let me say one thing for the cynics. No, i didn't do any of that so i could use it as an illustration. As i had already done it i just realised, as i was framing this chapter, that it could be an effective illustration to my point.

'Time spent together,' need not, and should not be diminished in a marriage. When apart we should really show our ingenuity within our relationship and love. Learn to passionately love from, or in, a different dimension.

Various researchers have identified certain key emotions as featuring more commonly when investigating the broader issues of the meaning of a successful marriage.[12] 'Companionship' and 'commitment' were the most common terms specifically mentioned. A distinct set of responses was often preceded with the phrase: 'it's about....' Then the subsequent comments were shown to fall into two primary categories.

The first set of comments referred to the concept of 'couple-ness,' for want of a better term, or the identity of the couple, such as doing things together, sharing, teamwork, joint and co-equal decision-making.

The second dimension identified basically encompassed the 'desired qualities' within a partner such as tolerance, supportiveness, tenderness, forgiveness and old favourites like communication.

So the deep need, to not only do things together, but to be together in a relational way, attached to supportive qualities translate to what most couples term intimacy.

Ted and beverley are missing true quality as expressed in the two areas above. Unless seriously and consciously corrected the situation and their marriage quality will only get worse.

Keep the desire of your intimacy high. Treasure 'togetherness.' Use absence to prove just how clever a 'lover' you really are.

---

12 Kaslow, Hammerschmidt, cited by Wallerstein and Blakeslee. The Good Marriage, Pub. Ticknor & Fields/Houghton Miffin Co. 1995.

Five

BEGGARS CAN'T BE CHOOSERS.

There are some things we should immediately confront head on. The phrase: 'Beggars can't be choosers,' is one of those soul-destroying statements that seriously need to be addressed. What a poor reflection of who we really are it conveys. I can remember growing up in a culture that often used that phrase.

What does it conjure up in your thinking? That you are a beggar! Now I'm sure we all have compassion for the homeless and those that end up on the streets begging, but let's deliberately confront this soul-destroying negative mind-set. And, confront it forcefully.

The image you have of yourself today exists because of the experiences of the past. Yes! However, the experiences of the past have not made you the way you are. They have however possibly made you believe you are the way you are. And it is in believing you are the way you are that indeed you are the way you are.

Never refer to yourself as a 'beggar.' Confront the 'beggar' mentality. You should be producing the Prince or the Princess in your relationship, not the beggar.

Consider the charming story of Beauty and the Beast. Here is a young girl who was not a Princess, not of royal, noble or aristocratic blood or background.

Yet, she, by uncompromising, self-sacrificing love, brought the Prince, the 'Best,' out of the Beast, the 'Worst.' That's the true model for marriage.

What are you producing the Beauty or the Beast? Do you have a poverty mentality towards your marriage, relationship, and spouse? Do you talk 'beggar' language that obviously suggests no positive, life-injecting choices? The old statement clearly implies beggars don't have a wide variety of options. I reject that thinking. Totally dismiss being typecast into a beggar mentality. We should actively reject not having the power of choice.

I choose to keep the relationship passionate, full of desire and like a new car optioned up with all the best extra features. I'm not thinking poverty of relationship with a fatalistic attitude: "Well that's the way it is. What can we do about it? After all, we're only poor self-defeating beggars."

Confront that rubbish. Change your mindsets. If you need to get professional help in dealing with the garbage of the past, then do so, but determine to have a great relationship as a Prince or Princess, not a beggar.

Understand that basically, the community has a poor mindset towards marriage as illustrated by a father whose son had just asked him what it cost to get married. "I don't know son. I'm still paying."

One elderly couple perfectly further illustrates corrupted mindsets towards healthy marriage. When they were asked what their secret to a long marriage was, their answer, though humorous, was tragic.

"Oh, we take time to go to our favourite restaurants two times a week. A little soft music, candlelight, beautiful food, and a slow walk home. He goes on Tuesdays, and I go on Fridays." Preserve us!

Graham and Contessa came from different cultural backgrounds. In courtship, they would occasionally lapse into disagreements that were more about their cultural differences than their relationship. Contessa had been raised in a culture and country where formerly women were not always appreciated for significantly more than their child-producing capacity, and their ability to work hard manual labour on the farm.

At twelve years of age Contessa had emigrated with her family. At twenty, as a student Contessa had met Graham whilst at university. Even going to university had raged as a continuing argument for months within Contessa's family.

"Girls don't need that. You gonna settle down and marry a nice boy from back home and make babies," Contessa's Mother said. Contessa cringed at her family's closed view of a woman's role in society, and their rejection of anyone not from their country of origin.

Her family was very restrictive about Contessa's growing relationship with Graham. Why couldn't she find a nice boy from home? (Meaning the country they had come from). Although Graham was a perfect gentleman he wasn't fully accepted because he was 'foreign.'

Isn't it a warped principle that one can emigrate from a different country and then call a young man, born in their land of residence, their adopted country, a 'foreigner.' Contessa however was not free from her own cultural hang-ups from her native land either.

At eleven years of age, just before emigrating, Contessa was seriously molested by her uncle and then raped by her eighteen-year-old neighbour six weeks later. Both men threatened to do terrible things to her family if Contessa ever said anything about their criminal, sick and sadistic violations. She had told no one – ever! Contessa determined never to marry anyone from 'back home.' So her past was creating flawed thinking and insecure grounds in looking for a life partner.

Because of the horrifying violations Contessa often, when she was having a bad day or experience, incorrectly saw herself as 'dirty.' Her self-esteem suffered. Contessa couldn't talk to anybody about the acts of sexual crime against her. She wouldn't dare. 'Nice girls' don't talk about such things. Slowly in her mind Contessa developed a 'beggar' mentality that she somehow wasn't worthy and had to just take her lot in life. What choices did she have?

Graham and Contessa married at twenty-five much to the pleas of Momma to wait for a nice boy from back home. Grudgingly her father gave her away on her wedding day. Both of Contessa's parents were sure she would come running back home when she really found out what terrible people Graham came from.

However, Graham was her saving grace. His gentle inspiring love changed her view of life. Graham treated her like a Princess, and used that term all of their courtship and afterwards. Slowly her false and incorrect feelings of worthlessness melted away in the arms, compliments, and attention of her lover, her best friend, and her husband who were all the same person. Soon, painful memories of violation faded.

Contessa's and Graham's passion, deep desire for each other and love continued after their marriage. At the suggestion of Graham's parents, they moved away from both sets of parents for 'social safety.'

They were just far enough away to return home every six weeks or so for a weekend and spend one night with Graham's parents and then one with Contessa's.

Even then, little things would spring to Contessa's mind as they spent the day with her parents. For Contessa's parents it was planned intrusion.

"Oh, I saw Carlos the other day," Momma said. "You remember Carlos? What a handsome man. Not married yet. Has two fruit shops now. You know ... Ahh..." Momma tailed off leaving very little to the imagination where she wanted the conversation to go. Contessa changed the subject.

Graham and Contessa had been very wise. In the final month of their engagement, they decided to create their own culture. Seeing they came from both a Spanish speaking and an English speaking culture they decided to create what they called a 'Spanlish' home. Nobody but them knew what it meant, but it worked.

Their home culture was a warm interaction of both cultures. It was a lovely balance of the best of both worlds. Happiness marked their relationship till around their tenth year of marriage. Graham was now working longer hours and Contessa was home with two children.

Though Graham never mistreated their relationship those special things he used to do to make her feel like a Princess slowly, very slowly dissipated away. The reference of the term 'Princess' dropped from his regular conversation usage. The past, the low self-esteem, the sense of worthlessness began to subtly and very slowly creep back into Contessa's thinking.

Once Contessa caught herself reflecting on it negatively. Because of the fatalistic culture she had been raised in Contessa heard herself one-day say: "Well, beggars can't be choosers." Contessa settled down to make the best of her life. Obviously, all her cousin's marriages were now dead boring, so why shouldn't hers be the same.

Graham slowly came to realise he was loosing his wife to lower motivations when Contessa sided with her mother on a weekend visit. Momma was ecstatic. Clutching the two grandchildren to her flour-coated apron, with Contessa at her side Momma glared at Graham, on the other side of the kitchen table and room, as some foreign intruder in the hallowed domain of her kitchen.

A thoughtful but lonely long walk along a picturesque valley path near their home was all it took to convince Graham. He, no they, needed help. Fortunately, the psychologist at his work was a personal friend to both Graham and Contessa. Slowly he probed and in the second session Contessa poured out the stories of the sexual violations as an eleven-year old. Graham sat stunned. He had never heard any of this before now.

As Contessa deeply sobbed Graham quickly moved to comfort her and hold her. "Come on Princess that's not your fault…"

Contessa didn't really hear much more of the torrent of loving affirmation that followed; she was caught up with his renewed use of the word 'Princess.' She was his Princess again.

It took a couple more sessions, but Graham and Contessa moved out of 'beggar' territory to the realm of Prince and Princess. Contessa realised she did have the power of choice. She eventually rejected rejection and chose choice.

Einstein, though not a good role model in marriage himself, is reported to have discovered that for every one negative input into our life, in a spoken word, it would normally take around eleven positive ones to wipe it out.

We now know that the average child in Primary School throughout the day receives from nineteen to twenty-one negative inputs to everyone positive one (from other children and adults). You do your own maths to see what would be necessary to wipe out all the destructive influences. Does it happen? No! So no wonder people struggle with self-esteem issues.

One researcher has shown that over 80% of children starting Primary School, in leaving the often-affirming environment of home, have strong self-esteem. However, by the time they reach High School, less than 10% of our incredible pre-teens and teenagers any longer have strong self-esteem. Sure there is a lot of bravado, but little healthy self-esteem.

So we must work on producing the Beauty, not the Beast. Continue the praise, affirmation, and edification of your partner to produce the best. You don't want to release the 'beggar' and all their 'choiceless' attitudes.

Six

MAKE HAY WHILE THE SUN SHINES.

Actually, you had better learn to make hay in every season of life if you want your marriage to succeed. Certainly, there will be better seasons in your life, more opportune times to fulfil your dreams and goals for marriage, but it is really in the 'dark clouded' times of your relationship that you can either develop true intimacy or begin to drift apart.

For those of you married, remember what you promised each other: "For richer, for poorer, for better, for worse. In sickness and in health..." Did we really mean those words, or were we so starry-eyed on that special day that we really didn't understand what we were saying, what we were promising? Be assured of this, tough time 'will' come. Also remember when the going gets tough the tough get going.

If you are committed only to 'making hay while the sun shines,' your relationship will be in serious trouble. Often, it is what is produced during the tough times, the sunless dark times that really builds a relationship. Sure, when everything is rosy and everything is sunny, then make hay to your hearts content. But, if you don't capitalise on developing intimacy during the 'darker' moments of life, your relationship will be the sadder for it.

Now lets stop a moment and briefly define terms. The word 'intimacy' to a woman means the warmth, openness and tenderness of the whole relationship, which includes sex in a balanced view. However, to a man it is more likely to mean firstly sex; secondly sex, and thirdly sex. So to be really helpful let us consider its use throughout this book from the broader, more balanced, female perspective. I think it is far more real, sane, and relationship-building (sorry guys).

John and Julie had been married for twenty-five years. Now in their early fifties their marriage was coming apart. In the formative years of marriage, they made a decision to be childless so they could work on their respective careers and capitalise on their finances. And capitalise they did. They became very wealthy.

Then in their late thirties and early forties they decided to have a family. Tragically, it was not to be. Even after trying for several years their referral to medical help proved fruitless. After several sessions with in-vitro-fertilisation, the fertility clinic's comment had not helped: "Oh, you've left it too long. We see this continually."

Referring to her passage through menopause Julie couldn't believe John's callous statement: "You'll get over it Jules. Every woman does. Just pull yourself together and stop getting so emotional. It's not like you. I can't take you anywhere lately." John clearly doesn't get it, does he? John scowled at Julie, who had tears in her eyes, as she disappeared into the master bedroom.

They filled their life with dogs, more wealth, horses, speedboats and social life. Sadly there was that missing factor between them. During those medical examinations, John seemed to Julie to grow a little distant. Why was he so resistant to gain medical help? Typical of many males John felt it intrusive for anyone to check on his sperm count.

Instead of them drawing closer through that experience, they began to drift apart. John immersed himself in more work, and Julie did the same, more as a reaction to John's withdrawal than a purposeful choice.

John as a company executive and vice-president required great analytical skills. Julie, on the other hand was a creative designer. How different they were. Their early fifties had brought them to crunch time.

Menopause began to take its toll early on Julie's body, her spirit, and her emotions. This once confident woman that as a creative business executive and co-owner of a fashion business was normally articulate, brilliant, innovative, creatively smart, and visionary was now reduced to tears at the drop of a hat. Her emotions swung so widely that Julie lost patience with herself, let alone John.

Instead of walking through this together and developing intimacy at a new level John headed for his cave, only he called it the office. He couldn't handle her mood swings. More sadly, John didn't care.

Isn't it sad that 'disinterest' can rudely push 'desire' right out of the relationship? How can couples let that happen? By not paying attention to keeping the relationship alive, second best takes over.

Here was a golden opportunity to build the relationship for John and Julie. Yet, they both let it drive and tear them apart. Gone was the desire or the passion to do anything about it. Disinterest reigned. Sexual intimacy started to seriously decrease, and Julie felt more used when John couldn't be bothered being close when she needed him, but was so very keen to exercise his 'marital rights,' as John so insensitively called it. As to fulfilling Julie sexually, well that seemed to stop years ago. It all appeared to centre on his sexual release.

Come back to the principal, and illustration, I referred to in the *Introduction* section. Do you think John is being confrontational in his marriage? Yes, if you mean confronting Julie over his false perception of what she's going through. Totally No, if you mean confronting himself.

Becoming confrontational with yourself makes a great marriage. "What can 'I' do to make this better for my spouse, to help solve this problem?" Challenging yourself, not your spouse is paramount. None of us have arrived at perfect knowledge or skills, so why avoid it? Maybe, just maybe, we need to change, to evidence that we want to keep the passion, desire, fun and spontaneity alive.

John and Julie have not developed opportunity through the tough times; they have developed resistance and rejection. For them sexual intimacy and growth have more to do with visions of their once youthful and nubile bodies than a gradual discovery of passionate, but maturing intimacy.

When will we learn that if we build, develop, and invest in the relationship on the non-sexual side of the bedroom door it will generally automatically keep alive the relationship on the sexual side of the bedroom door? We say this with an understanding of two reservations:

- *Firstly: something may have to be adjusted through therapeutic counselling in hurting psychological areas – eg: victims of sexual abuse or violation.*

- *Secondly: something physiological is going wrong affecting sexual performance or function in either partner. Again, an appropriate medical response is needed.*

Apart from these two issues the sexual side of the bedroom door will mostly take care of itself, if we are heavily investing in the non-sexual side of the bedroom door. In fact, there is nearly always a direct ratio of marital satisfaction hinging on this balance.

Sexual frequency is not the principle issue, but quality in the relationship is. However, an absence of sexual intimacy or an appalling low sexual frequency rate can be a source of concern. Professional help may be necessary to work through such issues.

Although, i'm sure that you would all realise that sexual frequency doesn't change with time in our marriage. Now, i can just about hear everybody yelling: "what planet is he on?" However, let me prove it.

Early in marriage sexual intercourse is generally what is termed 'tri-weekly.' After a few years it becomes 'try-weekly.' Later in marriage it becomes 'try-weakly.' See it never changes!

In the last ten or more years there has been an interesting change in the way we view, or should view, the phases of life we go through. In years gone by (and here we can safely say last century, even the last millennium), we used to view passage through difficult phases of the relationship as just something you had to get over.

Issues like pre-menstrual tension, post-natal depression, the birthing process, menopause, the male equivalent to menopause (andropause) or mid-life crisis, male propensity to stress and poor retirement adjustment were all things you had to 'get over.'

Sadly, often individuals didn't know how to respond proactively to them for good. So, instead of developing intimacy by both dealing with it positively together, we found individuals retreating to their corners waiting for the bell to ring, before they came out swinging at each other.

In the *introduction* section, we met sally and james. They clearly illustrated the point i am making. It is our total commitment and determination not to let these phases of life drive us apart and impoverish the marriage. The challenges of life should put determination into a dynamic marriage enriching it, instead of letting those issues create a disastrous marriage. We have to confront these 'dark days.' They will happen to all of us. No sun here to make hay. Importantly, we are determined to develop intimacy through it.

John could easily do what james did for sally. He could easily have found a top menopause specialist and with julie together attended appointments to bring the relationship through to a higher caring level. Further, john could have read on the subject. There are so many good books on menopause easily available today.[13]

Once, when i was referring to menopause and health issues in our *marriage, relationship seminar*, and responding proactively to it, i referred to the text reference in the footnote. A lady then asked from the audience: "i understand that's a secular book, can you refer me to a christian book on menopause please?" I looked at her with amusement and with a little mischief couldn't resist my cheeky response.

"Oh, i'm sorry, i didn't realize there was such a thing as a christian menopause and a non-christian menopause."

Sometimes we can get so stupid over issues. Just get help!!!

Sadly, john is too busy at the office. "She'll get over it."

---

13 As only one suggestion: The Silent Passage: Menopause, Gail Sheehy, Pub: Gallery Books, 2010 edition (Original edition goes back to early to mid 1980's)

Seven

Easy Come Easy Go.

A good marriage doesn't come easily. You have to work at it. Isn't it true that in courtship and early-married years we worked so hard on our relationship? It may have seemed easy to love that special one, but we put ourselves out. It didn't come easy. So why let it go easily?

Not caring that something is gone out of a relationship is frightening. It should never be 'easy go.' We should be really putting up a fight about losing any part of our relationship. It is never 'easy come,' and it should never be 'easy go.' That is the mindset of the indolent and the divorce fatalist.

This first aspect of 'desire' in building a great partnership focuses on keeping our desire and passion alive. Are we still valuing our beloved? Are we consciously still building up the love of our life, no matter how long we have been married? Do we still cherish them? Passionate people will say yes to each of these. Those wanting to keep the spark and intimate desire in their relationship know how important each of those areas is.

Mia was worried that Amar didn't seem to cherish her as he had once done in former years. Then, they would sit and talk for hours about everything when they were going together. Amar used to be such a good listener. Why had it now dropped out of their usual interaction?

Life was becoming boring. Their relationship was sadly and fastly slipping into a monotonous routine. As already stated one study has shown that women report that the two biggest stalers in a relationship are in fact routine and boredom.

Nothing was boring when they were twenty-one and newly married. Monotonous routine didn't exist. They were so spontaneous together. They would make love anywhere in the house. Now, they were lucky if it was twice a month, then always in bed, and definitely after the ten-thirty news.

Pauline and I speak in Marriage Seminars all over the world. We hit the sexual issue head on, because it is such a potential problem area.[14] Have you however heard about the speaker who surveyed his seminar audience concerning their sexual frequency patterns?

"Ok, all of you who make love three times or more a week put your hands up." People were horrified, giggled and squirmed in their seat. "Now come on, it's a normal biological function. Up with the hands." Slowly the giggling crowd complied. "Ok, how about twice a week?" The crowd slowly participated, still giggling. "Once a week?" "Once every two weeks? Now once a month?" He surveyed right down to once every six months.

Then, he began to share if it differed in various cultures, historical settings, age of partners, and so on (as it does). As he was speaking, a man up the back of the room began waving his hand.

"How can I help you sir?" asked the speaker.

"Well, sir, you didn't ask those who make love only once a year."

Stunned the speaker said: "Neither did I. However, is there anyone here that only makes love once a year?"

Now the same man at the back was furiously and energetically waving his hand. "Thank you," the speaker said. "But I don't think its that much to get excited about."

"Yes it is," cried the man, now out of his seat jumping up and down wildly. "Tonight's the night!"

---

14 Breaking Up: Separation And Divorce In Australia. Ailsa Burns, Thomas Nelson Aust. 1980, pp. 42-53. Highly respected lecturer at Macquarie University, Sydney. In her research she lists 'Sexual Incompatibility' as the No. 1 problem of couples causing breakdown of marriage.

Strangely Mia wasn't critical of Amar. She was acutely aware that now both just over thirty years old they had become predictable. Cherishing behaviours had all but gone. No longer did they seem to sit, talk, and just listen to each other.

One interesting study out of the USA found that couples who spent five to seven minutes relating together before they left the house (typically for work), in the morning, and similarly five to seven minutes reconnecting when they got home in the evening, were far less likely to divorce that couples who paid scant attention to the way they left or came back into the house.[15]

Good friends are glad to see each other, catch up, sit, talk, and share. Do couples lose that? Sadly, some people can spend more regular quality time and communication with a friend at work over coffee than they do with their own spouse. For many this has been the beginning of, and the breeding ground for an affair, when a person is revealing their emotional and empathy needs, and their regular coffee partner of the opposite sex is totally empathising. When this happens over an extended period 'empathy attraction' can replace spouse influence.

We often don't value something till we no longer have it. It's a sad situation where a man arrives home with a: "Hi, I'm home," planting a kiss on his wife's cheek as he walks past her, whipping up the paper and landing in the lounge room recliner with paper opened at the sports page and finger poised on the remote control to flip on the sports channel. Amazingly all of this was done on full automatic, all within ten seconds of the "Hi, I'm home." Oh, what a romantic chap.

Surely, we deserve better than that?

Amar came home late one Friday to find a note on the kitchen bench. "Gone away for the weekend to think things over. I'm sure you won't miss me. Mobile switched off. What has happened to us, and our marriage Amar? Back when I feel like it."

The note sent a chill down his spine. Anxiety and fear gripped him, not anger. The thought of not being able to contact Mia and not knowing her overall whereabouts and well being frightened him.

---

15 Survey by The Gottman Institute, Seattle/University of Washington – Tracked 658 couples over 14 years.

Culturally for Amar, this was unacceptable, but they were trying not to let their respective culture dictate their relationship. Though Amar didn't expect Mia to ring him, or answer his call, he left a message on her voice mail. He knew Mia would listen.

"Darling, please come home. I love you. Yes, you're right. We do need to do something about our marriage…." Amar could think of nothing more. He was numb.

As Amar sank down in the lounge chair all he could think of was the funeral of his boss's wife last week. Long would Amar remember Alec's words.

"I didn't get to tell her I loved her before she died. I left the house that morning annoyed about something that I 'thought' she had done. No kiss, no pleasant goodbye. Now she's gone with a sudden heart attack. And I didn't get to tell her I loved her…" Alec had broken down sobbing.

Early Sunday night Mia phoned. Tentatively she was checking out the lay of the land. Mia didn't want to walk into a fight. If so, she may as well stay away.

Amar responded with warmth, apologising that he had taken her for granted. Mia did the same; she was not looking to make him the problem.

Throughout the rest of that Sunday night, after Mia got home, till 1.00am on the Monday morning they sat and identified all the things that had once been their passionate joy, but had slowly slipped out of their marriage.

Openly and sensitively they acknowledged their own faults without needing to accuse each other. They agreed that their Indian ethnic background had made them more reserved about demonstrating their love openly in public.

"But we did love openly as young lovers," Amar offered. All Mia could do was smile.

Throughout the next four weeks they made a purposeful decision and agreed not to increase the sexual intimacy in their life, except totally ignoring the criteria surrounding the 10.30pm news. But, they worked on their emotional intimacy. They were convinced that the sexual side of their relationship would take care of itself, when they attended to the wider intimacy emotional support issues. This is always true. Passion, desire and spontaneity began to flood back into their relationship.

That long fifteen to twenty-minute cup of coffee together and chatting over the affairs of the day, when they first got home at night, started to hold special place in both of their hearts. Now, they could just share, just chat, just sit and listen. The world and its demands could go jump in the lake as far as they were concerned.

Amar and Mia began sharing the cooking of the evening meal. It further continued their meaningful conversation as they worked together. They developed a unique routine of adding to the meal's preparation without getting in each other's way. Amar focused on preparing the vegetables, salad, fruits and ingredient preparation. Mia concentrated on the finer points of mixing ingredients and actual cooking.

All of the time they were chatting, laughing and enjoying each other's company. Quality time started to become part of their daily routine, instead of a once in time wonder.

Eight

EASIER SAID THAN DONE.

Hugh didn't seem to be able to grasp that more was needed than words. Words he was good at. Actions were not his strong point. However, his words were not that life injecting either. Now in his mid fifties, with two grown up children with families of their own, it seemed all Hugh did was talk. Tragically, it was not healthy talk.

What does the old Hebrew proverb say: "Death and life are in the power of the tongue."[16] There's wisdom in those words. Unfortunately, if Hugh had ever heard them, he certainly didn't seek to speak life. The biting cynicism, accusations and blame that constituted his everyday words conveyed only death. Slowly, yet assuredly, their marriage was dying.

When Belinda had challenged him why they didn't have an exciting marriage any more Hugh came out with one of his usual tirades. "Well, it's more easily said than done."

"Great, that's just great. Here, I want to sensibly talk about 'us' and you launch off into well-worn rhetoric. The trouble with you Hugh is what you say is often rubbish and never loving or life injecting. And as for what's 'done,'

---

16   Proverbs 18: 21. For further Hebrew culture communication comment compare with Proverbs 13: 3; Proverbs 21: 23 and Psalm 34: 13.

as you call it…well, well, you never do anything." Belinda slammed the door on her way out.

People who know, very acutely, that you have to work very hard on both what is said and what is done, build great relationships. Actions do speak louder than words, but both should mirror each other. If our words don't speak life, then don't try excusing it with the flowers. If a man abuses his wife with physical or verbal abuse, then don't bother with any: "Well I really love you, but you make me so mad."

People are excuse machines. Challenge them and they have an excuse. We need to realise that we now live in a different world to grandma. In fact it's a new millennium, let alone century. Instead of constant excuses we should recognise that there are subtle changes occurring to the division of labour in the home. Child-care issues are changing. So too is the understanding of intimacy for men.

Most studies show women want more intimacy in the marriage. No guys I don't mean sex! They list intimacy and emotional support high in their 'need criteria.' Often, it is shown that these two areas are hardest for men to feel comfortable with.

Professor Lynne Segal[17] speaks of 'men's wretched fear,' of exhibiting the feminine qualities of dependency, intimacy, and closeness instead of being dominantly male.

Sadly, the men who often let women down by failing to validate them emotionally also tend to try and dominate them. Francesca Cancian argues[18] that women should accept that men's expressions of love, principally exhibited through practical help and sexual intercourse, is as valid as women's expression as evidenced through her need of emotional closeness and self-disclosure.

Who is right who is wrong – male or female? Neither! We are just different. Treasure difference.

Every time Hugh was challenged about the way he spoke to Belinda, and the state of his marriage there was always an excuse. "Well, you should see

---

17 Slow Motion: Changing masculinities, changing men. Lynne Segal, Basingstoke: Palgrave Macmillan, 2007.
18 Love In America, Francesca Cancian, New York: Cambridge University Press, 1987.

the house. It's enough to make a grown man cry. Why can't Belinda keep it tidy?" Hugh didn't bother to say the tidiness of his shed was an utter disgrace. Anyway, who said keeping the house tidy was only a woman's task?

Excuses and blaming one's partner are both cruel ways of not fighting fair. Every couple will have to sort out some issues. Resorting to excuses and blaming continually shows a total lack of accountability. Without accountability, no relationship can grow.

It is always very easy to blame another. This doesn't take any talent at all. Was Hugh always like this? No. As passionate younger lovers at university he would often compliment Belinda. She loved the way Hugh lifted her up with praise. They would have the occasional scrap like any couple, but he never resorted to blaming her or using lame self-protecting excuses. Hugh quickly accepted responsibility in their courting days and resolved the difference with genuine concern and apology.

Now tragically 'disinterest' dominated. Desire had seemingly taken a break, and apathy ruled.

When we don't keep passion and desire alive, true concern filters away. Then all that is left is not how to build our loved one, but how to justify yourself. Indolence is the opposite of passion. Excuses are the lifeblood of indolence. Disinterest replaces desire.

Did you hear about the devoted wife who had been by her husband's bedside every single day in hospital for several months as he hung between life and death? He kept slipping in and out of a coma, yet his wife was faithfully by his side. Eventually he slowly permanently came to. Seeing her by the bedside he motioned for her to come nearer.

As his wife stood by him, he whispered. She learnt over to listen, eyes full of tears. "You know what? You have been with me all through the bad times. When I got fired because of embezzlement you were there to support me. When I started a business and it failed because I wouldn't work you were right there. When I got shot by the debt collectors there you were, right by my side. When we lost the house because of my gambling, you stayed with me. When my health started failing because of drug taking you were still by my side. You know what?"

"What dear?" she gently said, eyes full of tears, smiling with a warm glow as her heart filled with a rewarding emotion.

"I think you're bad luck," he said.

Classic. Absolutely classic! Let's blame someone else, not be personally accountable – Yes that's really helpful, I don't think. Yet, those who are perpetual excusers and blamers are not passionate about their relationship. Their desire has been replaced by inert dullness.

Conclusion To: Desire, Passion, And Other Exciting Things.

Powerful relationships maintain passion. Their desire is much broader than sexual, though that is a powerful bond. It is relationship embracing. A certain element of fun and spontaneity mark the growing, maturing relationship, and couple.

Though their bodies grow old and maybe a little slower (not always), effective married couples haven't lost any of the 'twinkle' in their eye. They still use pet names. Wordless little gestures still hold the power they did in former years. They are in love.

Let me remind you again that both Pauline and I are not that impressed with the term 'falling in love.' As we've said, if you think about it, it sounds like a huge accident. We do however like the term 'rising in love.' It really conveys the true essence of a great relationship.

From the point when a couple meet, commit and ***yield to each other*** in marriage, there should be that rising and then even further rising of love. The traffic sign: *"Yield When Merging,"* really expresses a great marriage principle. Tragically, often for many it is the rise and fall of love. What we should be seeing is the rise and rise and continuing rise of love.

When we reach into the Fourth Dimension and make positive 'desire' choices, bolstered by a firm, immoveable, all-consuming 'determination' we can keep the passion and the desire area alive, no matter our age, or how long married. Never let 'disinterest' push aside 'desire.'

Hot passion and desire accompany the expression of young lovers. True! However, why should it dissipate with years married? We have to work hard at keeping desire alive. Every great relationship will do that.

Section 2

DECISIONS AND LIFE'S DIFFICULTIES.

Among many other upstanding integrity-driven Germans, Hitler incarcerated Dietrich Bonhoeffer, a famous Lutheran minister, into goal during April 1943. Under accusations of being involved in assassination plots against Hitler, Bonhoeffer spent two years in goal. Being goaled Bonhoeffer was not involved, as often thought, in the final failed bomb assassination attempt of July 1944.

Bonhoeffer was however, involved in early plans by members of the Abwehr (the German Military Intelligence Office) to rid Germany in assassination of the scourge and the insanity of Adolf Hitler, Nazism, and his associated evils. Charges of rescuing Jews and being aligned to the resistance were also levelled against him. Dietrich Bonhoeffer died courageously, by hanging on April 9th, 1945 at the Flossian concentration camp, at the hands of the Nazi warmongers, tragically just 23 days before the German surrender.

Bonhoeffer was to have performed the wedding ceremony for his niece, but because of his incarceration in goal could not. He wrote her a charming and inspiring letter of encouragement concerning her coming marriage that among other things contained these famous lines:

"Tis not love that will keep your marriage alive,
but, commitment that will keep your love alive."

Powerful thoughts. Sometimes a relationship requires a specific and deliberate decision to see things through. We are going to refuse to be petty and leave the marriage if we don't get our own way. No matter what comes against our marriage, we are not going to budge from being pro-marriage. We are not giving in. We're here for the long haul. We are committed 100%.

This is rarely an emotional response, though emotions are involved. Emotions may let you down, as we can sometimes not 'feel' like carrying on. We need a cold, calculated cognitive, or mental decision to press on, to love when we 'feel' unloved.

Through life's difficulties you have to resolve to hang in, oppose issues that are clearly trying to knock you off balance and make some courageous decisions about maintaining and fighting for the relationship.

These issues require choices, then positive determination to fulfil what we have committed our heart to. In fact, this is the testing ground, fulfilling the vows we made in our wedding service. These are the decisions for the long haul.

Healthy relationships do not come easily. They are costly. But, they are worth every effort put into fulfilling them.

One

A Wayward Apple Changes A Genius.

Isaac Newton strolled back to his favourite apple tree. It had been a while, too long, since he had been there for reflection, peace, and quiet.

"Oh, for five minutes peace," Isaac muttered as he sank down upon the soft emerald green grass, with occasional bright yellow buttercups showing throughout. He gazed at the fields below him. Then, he spotted the aging apple that had brought such insight to him when it struck him on the head many weeks ago.

He thought about that 1st law of relationship and smiled at the implications. Nobody would guess the double meaning in what Isaac meant by 1st law of motion, as the law would eventually become known as later published in his work *"Mathematical Principles of Natural Philosophy."* Since his last journey to the impressionable apple tree Isaac had observed further sad dealings with some of his friends, or more correctly their marriages.

Picking up the once-offending apple, now looking a little worse for wear, shrivelled and brown with age, Isaac hurled the aged apple backwards as far as he could from his position lying on his back on the soft grass and ground. Shrivelled apple remains disappeared over the brow of the hill behind him.

"Ow! What the heck." A wounded voice cried out from below Isaac's line of vision. Isaac sat bolt upright just in time to see Andrew, a stable-hand from the local manor, walking towards him rubbing his head.

"Hey, Andrew sorry about that. Bad shot hey?" Isaac yelled.

"Oh Professor Newton. Was that you? What ya doin? Experimenting on the locals?"

Both men chuckled as Andrew sat down next to Isaac.

"What a great day Professor," said Andrew shaking hands. "And how's life with you over at Trinity?"

"Ok I guess. But, tell me the last time I was here I could see a young couple having so much fun down there on the field, around the hay stacks. Someone later told me it was you. Who was the young girl?"

"That's no mere young girl Professor, that's the luv of me life. That's Joan. She's a maid at the Manor. Don't ya know her?"

Isaac responded with a smile: "Yes, I think I do, but not half as well as you by the look of things." Both men laughed. "Are you planning to marry her Andrew?"

"To be sure. But...," Andrew tailed off not immediately finishing his thoughts.

"What's up my man?" said Isaac. "Aren't you sure?"

"To be sure we are. But you see, her Mothers took ill and Joan may have to go care for her for a short while, and she's not sure what to do. Everything wus goin so well, but now this. But, Professor, yu know what, it only makes us the more determined. No matter what comes against us, we're gonna get married and stay as appy as we are now."

Andrew lay down, hands behind his head, with a long piece of straw in his mouth revolving in quiet circles as he chewed it. Wondrous thoughts of Joan filled his head.

Isaac Newton looked at his innocent friend. "Not sure it will always be that easy Andrew. I saw how much in love you are, but it takes more than love to keep a good marriage alive. Not that I'm an expert there." Both men smiled knowingly. "I'm watching the destructive evidence of that right now in some of my college friends."

"What ya mean governor? There's nuthin gonna take our love away. Who ya talking about?" Andrew was now leaning on one elbow towards Isaac Newton requiring, expecting an answer.

Isaac thought for a while, not wanting to use names, whilst thinking about John and Mary. "Well, I know this couple that has let their marriage get side-tracked. The man has become more and more involved in his work. His wife spends whatever time she can climbing the social ladder. They seem to have lost the fun and desire out of their relationship, like I see in you and Joan."

"How strange," responded Andrew. "How very strange. Why do ya think that's so?" he asked.

"Well," said Isaac scratching his head, "I think they've let their relationship get lazy. I'll guarantee once they had passion like you and Joan, but other things have now become their passion. Then there's this other couple…" Isaac thought for a moment. Would he mention Edward and Elizabeth by name? "…Well this other couple, he's done something really stupid and very wrong. He's being having an affair with a chambermaid at the manor. Now she's pregnant. Everybody's trying to hush the incident up but…"

"Ya, I know Professor, that's that idiot Edward. Sorry sir, I mean no disrespect to you. I'm just annoyed how he's wrecked the life of little Susie, though she was certainly foolish and not innocent herself. It's the talk of the village." Andrew eyed Isaac closely to see how he would respond.

Isaac said nothing. To him Edward was far more than an idiot.

"Things happen, Andrew. Circumstances often interrupt a once passionate relationship," Isaac commented as he lay down looking upwards through the dappled sunlight of the apple tree leaves.

"Excuse me governor, but that's nonsense. They've let lovelessness appen. Look see over there Professor," Andrew said pointing to a field to the side. Isaac sat up and both men stared at a small connecting field between two major village paths. "Look what's in the middle of the field. Ain't he a magnificent bull?"

Both starred at the impressive beast. The brown/red coat and white-faced Hereford bull was absolutely unique, the only one in the Cambridgeshire area, sent to see if the breed would be suitable outside the Herefordshire area. It had just been purchased from Herefordshire, where the breed was been newly developed in the late 1600's through to early 1700's. "Yu know Professor, Joan, and me often cross from one lane to the other right through that field. It's a short cut to the village."

"No. You're having me on," quipped in Isaac. "But, what of the bull?"

"Well, it's simple really. We gotta keep moving. In fact we gotta move faster than the bull. What's that I hear your students call it. What's that you're teaching them. 'Momentum!' That's it professor. We's got momentum in our relationship. No bull is gonna catch us."

Isaac fell about laughing at the thought of two young passionate lovers racing through the paddock, missing the occasional cow-pack and stinging nettles, outrunning and beating the new bull.

"The problem with your friends Professor, if I can suggest something, is they stopped runnin. They got na momentum. And the bull hit them fair and square. If you know what I mean." Andrew spoke forcefully, yet with gentleness as he starred at the imposing bull.

"Excuse me Andrew, I thought I was the professor. It seems to me that you understand about keeping a relationship alive better than my educated friends." Isaac gazed at Andrew expecting a response.

"Professor, the bulls will attack all of us. We alls got ta get from one point to another in our relationship. The only thing is we's got to keep the same passion, momentum if you like professor, in our marriage after we're married than before." Andrew paused waiting for Isaac Newton's response. Yet, there was none. He was deep in thought.

"The problem with Edward and Elizabeth, if you don't mind my saying, was Elizabeth thought he was still chasing her, when he had stopped a long time ago."

Isaac looked up smiling. "You're one smart man Andrew."

"Listen professor, the effect or impact of things that come along in our life and marriage will only be relative to the speed we're movin in our relationship. Edward and Elizabeth were standing still. The 'bull' clobbered them. Their fault, no one else's." Andrew carefully watched Isaac.

"Joan and me are gonna keep passionate, keep running so to speak. We just gotta make sure we always can run faster than the bulls, old ones or new ones. See ya Professor. Got to get back to work now." Andrew stood up shook hands with Isaac and strolled off back to the stables at the Manor.

Isaac sat there stunned after saying goodbye. Here was the missing key to his thoughts on relationship. He starred after Andrew then the concepts cleared in his thinking as he gazed for ages at the bull, standing serene and looking menacing – staring right back at him, snorting. Andrew had just rephrased Isaac's Second Law of Motion in relationship terms. How brilliant.

"Now, I can't just go on talking about outside forces attacking relationships. It's not proper in the 1680's. What shall I call relationship, I know I'll continue to call it a 'body,' and I need to think again in terms of motion, and align it with my Second Law of Motion to disguise my discovery." Isaac stood up, leant against the apple tree and watched the bull. "I've got it!"

"***An outside force*** (like the bull or as in Edward's case adultery), ***acting on a body*** (relationship and marriage) ***causes the body*** (relationship and marriage) ***to accelerate in the direction of the line of force*** (eg: the bull's butt! The direction of the force)." Isaac roared laughing. "Brilliant, brilliant." Isaac was now jumping up and down with excitement. He stopped. "Wow!" He settled down and grabbed something to write on to record his thoughts.

"***Further, the acceleration is directly proportionate to the force*** (the 'bulls' of life) ***and inversely proportionate to the mass of the body*** (relationship and marriage)." [Laws Of Motion No. 2]

"Now, I can't call this my 2nd law of relationships. Better continue calling it my 2nd law of motion." Isaac walked off quickly towards Trinity College desiring to expand his thoughts. Isaac could see the principle clearly now as it related to marriage.

Every relationship has not only to keep moving, but also, keep the passion, desire and 'momentum' as Andrew called it. Clearly Andrew understood 'things,' pressures, and challenges will happen in every marriage, but they have least effect on those marriages maintaining passionate momentum, and most effect upon those whose relationship had stalled. They are the ones who get clobbered by the 'bull.'

Clearly Andrew saw this as a cognitive choice, a specific mental decision about commitment to keep the relationship alive, despite what may come.

> ***The Challenge:*** *Have you made a conscious commitment, a mental decision, to keep the marriage, and relationship passionate and moving? Can you see and further define the potential bulls in life? Does your relationship move passionately faster than the bulls? Such positive responses need to be your decisions. It is a personal choice based on awareness.*

Two

BETTER TO GIVE THAN RECEIVE.

If taken to an extreme, have you ever heard of such a potentially relationship-destroying statement? It doesn't take much imagination or intelligence to figure out what will happen in any healthy marriage relationship if all you're ever doing is giving, giving, giving, and never receiving anything back in return. You can only give so much without some loving reciprocal action returned, before you start to feel used.

Great intimacy is kept alive because of an integrated dynamic of both giving and receiving. Conversely, if we only live to get, then our relationship will also be headed for trouble.

Graham's work psychologist, after several sessions, began to challenge Graham and Contessa towards deeper levels of commitment. "Look, you guys have made tremendous progress. You really have. It is great to see that spark, passion and fun within your marriage again. However, renewing passion and desire is only one level in a healthy relationship. Many can regain it, but constantly slip back into old habits because they don't go to the next level."

Graham cut in. "Well Joe, what is that level? We don't want to go back to where we were before. We're so appreciative of rekindled love." Contessa smiled, happy to have her man back in full swing in the marriage. She no longer found Mills & Boon books that interesting.

"It is simple, but hard. Commitment is a decision. It's the unmovable, solid 'never-give-up' decision and calculated commitment that is necessary to see you through the ups and downs of family life." Joe continued to share principles on decision-making and commitment, encouraging Graham and Contessa's participation in discovering new truths.

Few couples just stop, all of a sudden overnight, doing wondrous things for each other. Decreasing loving ways generally happens gradually. Like a slow leak in the tyre, it will let them down eventually. Slowly key intimacies and loving actions that are the glue in a relationship, or the grease to the axle preventing friction, slowly slip out of daily interaction and before we know it we're boring.

Solid decision-making and commitment, no matter how we feel, has to be sown into the equation. We practise such actions on other levels why not in marriage. Sometimes we may not 'feel' like going to work, but we do. We may not 'feel' like getting the weekly shopping done, or washing the laundry, but we do. Things would certainly grind to a halt if we didn't.

Contessa found herself responding in every way to Graham as she saw he had deliberately made a choice to be proactive in the repair of the marriage. As they drove home that day they discussed Joe's concept of decision-making and commitment.

"Giving is a two-way street," Contessa offered. "The more you give; the more I respond in kind. What is it your Mother says: 'what you sow, you will reap.' However, what Joe's saying is instead of that being a spontaneous gesture, which is good; we need to make a mental deliberate decision about our commitment to giving to each other. Rather than giving being optional, it should be naturally mandatory."

"Well honey, you can keep on giving to me. I love your giving in the bedroom and out. Those special dinners – umm, umm!" Graham offered as he got a playful slap from Contessa.

However, Graham realised that things like touching without sexual con-notation, listening and small gifts were very important to Contessa. Graham changed his thinking from it would be pleasant if they happen, to: "I've got to make a decision to make loving actions happen. Yep! I need to pop a note in my diary to occasionally buy those little gifts Contessa just adores."

Even when life's challenges occur that can threaten the relationship, like illness, pressure with children and the like, when we have made a strong decision-making commitment, we will follow through. We need to commit to small things like small meaningful personal gifts and deliberate thoughtful gestures and words.

Now, I have it on good authority guys, that none of the ladies will stop you spending any money on them. Understand however that you don't always have to spend money to creatively love.

You could pick a beautiful rose or other flower from your own garden as you come home from work and lay the rose/flower on her pillow with a little note saying: "I love you." This can mean so much.

The gift of time together, a creative candlelight dinner at the park or beach, setting up candlelight illuminated scented bubble bath for your wife, so she can soak and relax for a time, whilst you mind the children, may take nothing more than thoughtfulness – good creative thought. Before anything else, loving is a decision.

Most of us were great at giving when we were courting. Why lose such a benefit because we are married? Interestingly, most of our gifts when courting were either things we did, or relatively inexpensive but thoughtful gifts. We often didn't have a lot of money (I know, you might say: "Hey, nothing's changed"), but we did have a creative urge to love, bring pleasure and happiness to the one we were keeping company with. Why change what worked?

I remember an incident when I was in the USA for eight days on speaking engagements before Pauline joined me. Pauline had some speaking commitments herself in Sydney that delayed her initially travelling with me from the beginning of our USA itinerary.

Before Pauline was due to fly into Muskegon airport in Michigan, I had gone to the florist and bought four helium 'I Love You' balloons and loose rose petals. The balloons were tied to the four corners of the bed. The rose petals were sprinkled from our hotel room door to the bed.

What did such actions cost? Actually, very little except a decision and commitment to keep gifts, giving and love alive. Make a decisive commitment, even in times when you don't 'feel' like it.

Interestingly, Pauline later gave the four balloons away to four couples in the Marriage/Relationship Seminar we were doing in that community three days later. We knew we couldn't travel by air with them to our next appointment. You'd think 'Christmas' had arrived for the four couples they were so excited about their balloons. Bringing joy doesn't cost that much.

Listening is definitely a commitment. When difficulties have the potential to put their head up then we need to remind ourself of our commitment to listen.

One interesting study in the USA[19] found men in speaking use from nine to twelve thousands words a day. However, women use from twenty to twenty-four thousand words a day. Figures cited for both sexes often vary slightly.

One man, lacking in any sense, or discretion, in the midst of a serious difference with his wife about him not listening to her showed her these statistics in a magazine article.

"See, see, you women use twice as many words as we men do," the husband yelled. As if that justified him not listening.

His wife sceptically eyed off the statistics, quickly reading the article. "Well, you know why that is don't you?"

"No, why," he snapped back annoyed.

"Well, it's because we have to repeat ourself all the time."

He stared at her vacantly. "Pardon," was his only reply.

Let's make a commitment to listen, to just have 'us' time, where we can just share and listen. Turn off the TV for a period. Listen to each other as you go for a walk. Our fast moving technological 'IT' world is gradually desensitising us to attentive, sensitive listening. Often, if we're not being entertained, we're not effectively listening. Don't fall into that trap.

Contessa knew how much touching meant to Graham. She made a personal commitment to be more open to his needs. Contessa thought about

---

19 This is what is called the: Louann Brizendine's Assertion, from her book: The Female Brain. Pub: Morgan Road Books, 2006. Brizendine is a neuropsychiatrist.

how she had complained that Graham only seemed to be sensitive to touching in the bedroom. On reflection Contessa realised she wasn't initiating outside the bedroom either.

Graham appreciated Contessa's decision and commitment and realised that touching to a woman doesn't always need to lead anywhere. Touching is therapeutic in itself. A hug to a woman needn't always lead to the bedroom. It's part of her security system and need. Now note I didn't say wouldn't, I just said needn't.

Commitment, genuine decision-making commitment didn't come easy to Contessa and Graham, and neither will it to you. But, commitment is vital in the difficult times, the 'I don't feel like it' times. This resolve is so essential, so powerful in our relationship. Both Graham and Contessa began to appreciate that both giving and receiving are just the two sides to the same coin.

Three

Don't Put Off Till Tomorrow, What You Can Do Today.

I fully understand the impact of the proverb/adage above, but some vital issues in our life will take the 'tomorrows' to see them come to pass. Remember as courting couples how you would sit and talk, and talk, and talk. More importantly you listened.

Amid the many things you shared was a component of dreams and goals. Probably we didn't see them as dreams and goals back then, but they were there, nevertheless.

"Oh, isn't it going to be wonderful when we grow old together, seeing our children grow up and married with children of their own. Ah, grandchildren! Won't it be exciting to retire together in a beautiful natural stone-built home inclusive of a real fireside and stone chimney, with cedar decking right around the house? Let's build it up in the valley overlooking the sea, with a lovely white picket fence all around it, and a garden full of beautiful red and white roses." And on we went.

Dreams, goals, and vision are vital to a growing partnership. If you aim at nothing, you're sure to hit it. I'd rather get to 80% of something than 100% of nothing. Pauline and I set goals. We have over the years developed them for several key areas of our life and work. However, the No. 1 area has always been our marriage and our family.

Keep in mind you can dream about something or go out and make those dreams happen. Go out and make happy marriage happen.

The total fulfilment of some major goals I must put off till tomorrow. Maybe it will take five or ten years to fulfil a goal – eg: Pay off the mortgage early and be debt free. But, if you don't put in place mini-steps, to fulfil your goal you may never arrive and see it completed.

The most important goal structure in life to Pauline and I is what we call your 'micro-goals.' They are in reality your smaller strategies and steps to reach your goal. This is your decision today to do something about reaching the ultimate goal. Micro-goals are something you must do 'now' for the 'to-morrows' to be fulfilled.

Be prepared for success, or else you could get caught out. Consider the man who was a keynote speaker at a banquet and in his haste to get to the engagement forgot his false teeth. As he sat at the head of the table, he realised his dreadful mistake. Turning to the man sitting next to him he said through a gummy mouth, and difficult pronunciation: "I can't speeek two nite, cause I've four gotten my teef. I can't even eat dinner."

"No problem," said the man, "try these." He discretely pulled a set of false teeth from his pocket. Gratefully the man took them and tried to hide as he put them in, half hiding below the table edge. "Too tight," he said whispering. Not deterred the helpful dinner companion discreetly whipped out a second pair. "Try these."

The speaker tried them and responded: "No, too loose." Not fazed at all the man pulled a third set of teeth out of his pocket.

"They're perfect," said the speaker after he tried them, head now above the table. With that he gratefully ate his dinner and then gave his banquet speech. After the dinner meeting was over he went over to thank the man who had helped him. "I want to sincerely thank you in coming to my assistance. It was lucky I was sitting next to a prosthodontist and dentist."

"Oh, I'm not a dentist," the man replied. "I'm an undertaker."

Maybe the way we should look at our proverb heading is as follows: 'Project for tomorrow the major goals of your life, but ensure they are reached by fulfilling micro-goals each day, which draws that final goal closer and closer, sooner rather than later.'

Though the following illustration is illuminating some may take offence, if they choose to misread its motive. Watch how you interpret, or more correctly apply it.

A study in the USA[20], found that in a very large survey field, across a wide range of demographics 24% of the research group had no idea of what the future would hold for them. They literally had no goals. Another 60% had only a vague idea. 'Oh, in 5 years time I think I might be married.' 'I might have a better job I suppose.' A further 13% had strong mental goals. 'Oh, that's easy. In 5 years time we would have purchased our first home. I'll be the head of my department. I'll...' However, only 3% had well defined 'written' goals.

Now listen to the extension of study, many years later, on the majority of these same individuals. When they surveyed them again the results were staggering. Of the 24% without any goals, nearly all of them were on Social Welfare.[21] The next 60% were all averaging the basic wage or just more, whilst the defined 13% were earning up to three times the basic wage. Consider the 3% that were interestingly different. They were the wealthiest of all.

Take such an illustration as you will, but let it inspire you to have goals. Further, break your goals down in bite-sized pieces and develop some micro-goals or strategies today to launch you and your relationship towards success.

To illustrate, let us say you had as a long-term goal to pay off your house in 15 to 18 years instead of original set 25 years. Now you need some 'micro-goals.'

As a micro-goal you could deliberately purpose to put all your loose change, out of your pocket or purse, in a jar, or tin on the kitchen bench every night. Guaranteed at the end of the year you will have enough at least for an extra house repayment.

Secondly, you could say to yourself: "Every time I get a coffee I'm going to put the same amount aside as saving in my kitchen bench jar/tin. I shouldn't

---

20 What They Don't Teach You At Harvard Business School. Mark McCormack. Pub: Lifemastering. 2006. He investigated a study of 'Goal-Setting' at Harvard MBA program in 1979.

21 Here is where you can react if you choose. The fact is welfare is valid and a necessary form of support to meet the needs of those in crisis and we should be both sensitive to those needing it and appreciative of its provision.

let coffee drinking use all my spare money." Again at the end of the year you could have a further substantial amount to pay off the house.

Now if I said to you: "Just pay an extra payment off your house each year," you would probably tell me: "Impossible. The budget is too tight." But, that loose change every night and the extra coffee money challenge seems so insignificant, yet can add up to a minimum of at least another house repayment. You can do it. You just have to find workable 'micro-goals' and action them.

With an extra one, one and a half or two house repayments a year paid against your house loan you will be amazed at how that will *radically* reduce the life of the loan. Your decision, and absolute determination to follow through, on your 'micro-goals,' on a day-to-day basis, has helped you reach the decision of your main goal.

Let us take a look at Tony and Cheryl again. Tony has privately set a goal to get to their golden wedding anniversary and be as deeply in love as they were when they first married. He shared his goal with Cheryl, and she decided to take up the same challenge and goal. Now, they knew they had lost a little momentum from their marriage, but bravely set their goal and created micro-goals to reach it.

Tony had become acutely aware that he can immerse himself in work, and their relaxing time together can get pushed aside. So Tony sat down and made a weekly and monthly diary entry. For Tony a creative idea had to be a diary entry; otherwise, he would forget. Tony would forget not because he didn't want to reach his goal, but a day can become a week, can become a month, can become six months, and can become a very bad habit.

Once a month to six weeks maximum Tony planned on doing something special, often going away for the weekend with Cheryl. Weekly for Cheryl he planned to do something quite spontaneous. Though the idea is planned for him, it is spontaneous for Cheryl. Last week Tony had to work back on his scheduled rostered once a month late shift. Tony had left a note on Cheryl's pillow. "Be ready at 10.00pm, glad rags on. We're going out for supper when I get home. No hints, just a surprise."

Coffee and cake at the city's revolving 24-hour restaurant overlooking the city and inland lakes didn't cost that much. Yet for Cheryl she was sitting on top of the world.

Cheryl also had implemented her own micro-goals. Realising their relationship had staled a little Cheryl had more and more pulled away from Tony sexually. The passion of their first years of marriage had sadly gone. Sexual frequency even started to worry her. It was very apparent such worried Tony. He said so in no uncertain terms in one of their fights, before they addressed changes in their marriage.

Now, the tables were turned. Now, Cheryl had a solid decision-making commitment to return the passion and desire to their relationship. She started her crusade of implementing her micro-goals. Saving a little every week from her personal allowance in their budget Cheryl bought beautiful new lingerie.

As Tony was reading a book in the lounge room one Wednesday, just after lunch, Cheryl slipped off to shower, changed into her new 'secret weapon' and came back just to the lounge door. Their grown children were at university, one now married, and Tony on a rostered day off.

"Honey." That's all Cheryl had to say as he looked up. Tony got the message. The book hit the floor with a bang as he pounced over the lounge and began chasing her, as she ran screaming and giggling hysterically towards the bedroom.

Making sure their children weren't coming over for a visit one Saturday afternoon Cheryl called Tony from the bedroom. As he turned into the hall there was a trail of skirt, blouse, slip, bra, panties, suspender belt and matching stockings.

With a Tarzan cry, beating his chest he yelled out: "Me Tarzan, you Jane," as Tony burst into the room to find Cheryl waiting in bed for him, laughing at his antics.

Both Cheryl and Tony made some decisions then set some goals, then micro-goals, but more importantly resolved to make a solid commitment towards them. They recognised the necessary small steps to reach the major goal and put them in place.

For Tony, a diary entry was necessary. For Cheryl, creative ideas were something she could easily remember.

Who did it right? Neither. They both fulfilled their goals. Both deliberately illustrated their commitment and such was fulfilled.

It is unfulfilled expectations that always lead to emotional distance and potential disaster. We all will face difficulties at one time or another. Life can be cruel and hard.

It's our resolve; our conscious decision-making to succeed that makes us come through. One interesting anonymous study of eighty-one strong families showed how they coped with a severe crisis.

23% of the families cited serious illness or surgery as the most difficult crisis they faced together. 21% of the families identified death in the family. Interestingly, marital problems ranked third.

Amazingly 96% of the families were found to have successfully met the crisis. A primary contributing factor was 'pulling together, rather than apart.' Crisis should bring us to a new level of 'togetherness' and commitment, not destroy us.

Gottman[22] in a video documentary refers to this 'pulling together' in a different way as he talked about 'The Masters Of Relationship' and 'The Disasters Of Relationship.' He was referring to 'Sliding Door Moments' where you can take either of two possible choices. It is established that physically, mentally, emotionally and socially literally turning towards each other, not drawing away was extremely important. Gottman indicating that research showed in the midst of tension, problems, and marital crisis 86% of 'The Masters' literally and figuratively turned towards each other. However, only 33% of 'The Disasters' similarly turned towards each other.

Let us take on the challenge of finding the opportunity in the crisis. In the Chinese pictographic writing system, the Chinese symbol for the word 'crisis' is a composite picture linking their symbols for 'danger' with the symbol for 'opportunity.'

There lies great truth.

---

22 http://vimeo.com/22979893 doco.video: After Happily Ever After. Included interview with John Gottman as per above.

Four

NEVER A LENDER, OR A BORROWER BE.

What planet was the individual on that created that proverb? Now, I clearly understand how much trouble unregulated money and mindless credit use can cause in a marriage, but to never lend, invest, or be generous – give me a break. Borrowing may cripple you if you don't work out your financial capacity and then stick to a well-developed written budget you have worked on together. Nearly all of us purchase our home using borrowing.

In no particular order money, children, allocation of time and sex are the top four issues cited by couples that they fight about. Money is clearly represented. Now in the majority of cases few of us as children or teens were specifically taught how to budget, handle money, and certainly hardly any of us were constructively taught how to handle credit.

Money drives much of our motivations – for good and bad. A wife upset with her husband said: "I think you only married me because my Daddy left me lots of money."

"That's not true," defended her husband. "I didn't care who left you the money."

Often, we blame each other about the way we handle money, but finance has to be a joint responsibility. A husband upset with his wife's spending on the weekly groceries said: "Where on earth does all the grocery money go?" Not fazed at all his wife replied: "Turn sideways and look in the mirror."

Money; often you can't live with it, and you certainly can't live without it. How the form and patterns of money use have changed over the past forty to fifty years.

Within Australia the 'plastic/credit card' money era arrived in 1972, and was ultimately released in 1974.[23] We did have credit systems before that with lay-byes, time payment and higher purchase, but 'plastic' – the credit card – arrived and changed the world.

Within Australia around 1973, 1974 the average Australian home saved between 16%-17% of the weekly wage or salary, and remember there were far more one-income homes than now. Yet today, because of our credit lifestyle and often enslavement to credit cards, Australians save less than half a per cent. More and more women are working, not merely for their sense of fulfilment (which is good), but essentially to make ends meet as we nationally sink further into debt.

How did great grandma get a new fridge? She saved up for it. No money – no fridge or other goods. And remember usually only great grandad worked. Today, plastic has changed the face of how we use money. The trouble is credit debt brings with it sociological pressures that are seriously disturbing family life, generally initially upsetting marital harmony.

In the United Kingdom, it is conservatively estimated one in ten households are having trouble repaying debt. For every credit card owned ten years ago, there are three in its place today. Financial debt however has more than trebled.

You might say: "That's obvious. If they have three cards to one from ten years ago, surely their debt would have trebled." That's the sort of thinking that gets us into serious financial trouble. If you can afford a $4,000 limit on your credit card and have factored a substantial repayment amount each month into your budget, what makes you think you can afford more than $4,000 whether you have one, three or ten credit cards? With multiple cards, the danger is people often maximise them each out to $4,000. Now they're in serious trouble.

---

23 Oct. 1974 saw the launch of Bankcard [www.bankcard.com.au/history.htm]. Bankcard

The average UK family will be carrying (not paying off) credit card and store card debt of more than 3,000 pounds. In Australia the Reserve Bank conservatively puts credit card debt at around $3,500 per card, or $4,500 per credit card holder.[24] You can often double that figure for a husband and wife. With many individuals having multiple cards the debt escalates. The national credit card debt for 22 million Australians as at Oct. 2013 was $36 billion.[25]

Imagine what a 'blow-out figure' this is likely to be for those who owe money on their cards, after you take out the number of cards where people pay them off totally before any due date, and the number of people who don't own or refuse to own credit cards.

Pauline and I have three credit cards, only consistently using two, but we carry no debt on due dates for payment as the cards are always paid off in advance. Both Pauline and I refuse to pay interest. We use credit; credit doesn't abuse us!

In the UK[26] debt help lines report the average credit debt per adult is 28,630 pounds (so for a couple double that figure). Consider that is every adult in the country. Think about what debt some would be carrying with a reasonable percentage of adults with houses paid off and no credit card debt, alongside those renting and not having a mortgage, not that mortgage was always part of this credit debt. Also in the UK more than 300,000 people are currently overdue on the mortgage by more than three months. Every year in the UK three million summonses is issued for personal debt recovery.

It is disturbing that in the UK 164 million pounds is charged in interest daily on all national credit and every 17 minutes and 4 seconds a property is repossessed. Every 5 minutes someone is declared insolvent and personal debt in the UK stands at 1.427 trillion pounds. Welcome to credit and its traps.

The bottom line is if you don't learn to handle money wisely debt will handle both you and your relationship poorly.

Good money management was not Hugh and Belinda's strong point. They have never purchased their own home, always renting. Not that either

---

24 www.moneysmart.gov.au/borrowing-and-credit/credit-cards/credit-card-debt-clock
25 Ibid.
26 http://themoneycharity.org.uk/debt-statistics as at Oct. 2013.

Hugh or Belinda didn't earn good wages, it was that they just couldn't control their spending. They had little in savings.

When Hugh, a company executive, came home with a new jaguar leased on a special fleet-owner deal; Belinda was furious. Hugh had not even discussed getting the car with her. "Well, heck, you know I have to keep up appearances with my job," Hugh screamed after her as Belinda disappeared into the bedroom.

"How, on earth are we going to afford that now, we're already up to our eyeballs in debt," Belinda yelled as she slammed the bedroom door.

Half an hour later Belinda had a solution. She was off to the shopping mall to do some shopping. "Why should he have all the fun?" Belinda muttered as she again slammed the front door. Unfortunately Belinda often slammed doors.

By late afternoon, Belinda's plastic credit cards were almost too soft to use because her cards had overheated repeatedly running through charge card machines.

There are some issues in a marriage you should make specific conscience decisions about. Money is one of those things. Hugh and Belinda may never own their own home, as a capital asset, given the poor money management they exhibit. They don't even have a written budget.

All of us as couples need to make a sensible, head-operating decision, that we will manage money well. If you don't your relationship will be the poorer for it. You need a well defined written budget.

Hugh and Belinda mentally decided a budget would be good. Sadly 'decision' became 'deferment' as a day became a week, then became a month, then tragically became a lost idea and indecision.

Belinda, as a professional, had returned to work once the children were mid-teens. Together Belinda and Hugh's combined wage would put them in the top 10% of family incomes in the country. Now in their mid fifties they normally should have paid off a house with their income level and also have one or two investment properties. However, spending is out of control with both of them. And, they each blame the other.

"Belinda, why on earth do you need another five blouses that's ridiculous," shouts Hugh as he waves the credit card statement in the air. There he stands, in his $275.00 shoes Hugh bought on credit on Friday. Tonight, they will be taken off and set alongside his twenty other pair of shoes – all 'very' expensive.

"Yeh, what about those shoes?" Belinda throws back.

"They're not on this credit card statement," says Hugh angrily waving the statement at Belinda. No, Hugh, they're not. Interestingly they will be on next months, won't they?

Money is not one of those subjects you should deal with in the heat of anger. Finance and budgets have to be settled in the cold light of a calm day. Have you created a budget that includes the concept and use of credit cards and other credit facilities? There are several good books you can get at a reasonable sized bookstore on money management, budgeting, and associated financial issues.

I highly recommend the book: *'The Richest Man In Babylon.'* [27] Most 'good' bookstores will have this, or can easily order it in. Ignore totally the fact that the original print came out in 1926. In its defence (which is totally unnecessary once you read it), let me say the book is more up-to-date than tomorrow's Financial Times. If you would put in place the recommendations and philosophy of this easy to read book you ***will*** truly be in charge of your money and not the other way round. My copy is a 1988 imprint. In 1988, there had been sales of over two million. Today, nearly twice that figure is accepted. An updated version for the 21st C is available. Well worth the read.

If necessary find a financial counsellor or company and allow them to assist you resolve the issue of money management. Learn, because finance management is an acquired skill. To manage your money, budget, and handling the credit card/s takes time purposefully given to learning. Managing money takes specific decision-making, determination, and resolve to stick to your commitment.

Allow one point of advice. Refinancing may sound attractive, but remember its exponents will always profit at your expense. Be careful if you use it. I'm not totally against it, but it must ***absolutely and definitely*** address one key issue. If those assisting you refinance don't address the issue: 'Why you're in a financial mess, and are over your head in credit debt, and what to do to

---

27 The Richest Man In Babylon. George S Clason. Pub: Signet Book (Penguin Group). 1988 (later imprints exist).

stop this,' then expect further problems. You must change how you handle money, especially credit, from that point onwards. If you don't statistics show you'll be in a worse financial position in 5 to 7 years than you were before you refinanced.

Certainly use credit, but don't let credit abuse you.

For the sake of stable, tension-free marriages, I would as a personal recommendation suggest that you bring your credit cards to a zero balance at the end of each month. The banks/credit institutes don't get a single cent out of Pauline and I in interest, but we get all the benefits of a free credit time, the frequent flyer points and other rewards.

If you must have a credit balance that you're paying off, '*never*' pay them the 'minimum payment due' figure on your statement. Scott Pape, a media financial commentator[28] gives an illustration of a fully 'maxed' out credit card at $4,500. Given the current interest rates of early 2014, if you only ever paid the minimum payment due month by month, and never ever added any further debt to that card, then it would take you thirty-one years to pay the debt off. Tragically Pape reported that 85% of Australians generally only pay the minimum payment due. No wonder on an average credit debt is such a crisis to people, and such a money maker for the banks.

If you must owe on your card/s make sure you include in your overall budget a credit card/s repayment figure that will be at least three to four times the 'minimum payment due' amount on a fully-maxed out card. Make that a budget item. Then make a sensible decision to *only* ever use your credit card/s for items *actually in your budget*, so they are paid off at the end of the month with allocated budgeted money.

With the above philosophy, you will be out of credit-card/store-card debt very soon. Make money work for you, not the other way round.

Understand also that family life in general will mean a change and a challenge to our money usage.

A 1997 study found that a first child coming into the home was associated with a decrease of about or at least $162,000 in after tax, and after

---

28 Scott Pape, Channel Seven (TV) 4.00pm News, 21st February 2014, Sydney.

expenses lifetime earnings. The research assumed here that the wife does not return to work thereafter. This has dropped from the suggested 1986 figure of $435,000. However, consider that their initial 1986 research was based on also including a full higher educational or university degree level education for children.

Having children brings money pressures. It is just part of life. Adjust wisely to money together or let bad money management rip you apart. The choice is yours.

Five

BUSINESS BEFORE PLEASURE.

Who says we can't have pleasure whilst we're attending to the more 'business' side of who we are as a couple? I know that in this Section we are looking at decisions and life's difficulties, but we ought to approach them with joy, fun, and a good sense of humour.

Surely, we want to emphasise the cold hard decisions and commitments we will be making in the relationship, but that doesn't, shouldn't, and mustn't exclude pleasure.

Living together with another human being long term requires severe and necessary adjustments. Are we committed to the process? We all live in a self-indulgent world that cares little about the next person. Only if your insane would you carry this attitude into marriage.

'Selfies' is the in-term expressing this self-indulgent age. The term has even gained a place in the Oxford Dictionary. Take that self-centred attitude into your marriage and I'll guarantee you will bump into severe problems.

Have you heard about the extremely self-centred little girl?

'I had a little tea party, one afternoon at three.
Though very small, three guests in all, just I, myself & me.
Whilst I ate up the sandwiches, myself drank up the tea.
Twas also I who ate the pie, and passed the cake to me.'

Sadly many individuals can live at that level in their relationship. The choice is ours to be a 'giver' or a 'taker.' I think certain things become conscious resolves that we need to make (decisions if you like), but their outworking brings much pleasure into the marriage.

Acts of devoted service towards your loved one fall, in my estimation, into that area of conscious decision-making and commitment. The business end of the relationship needn't be boring. Though they may create great pleasure, they were spawned by a solid resolve: "This is what I must do and enjoy doing to keep my relationship alive."

To me these acts of devoted service are part of the 'random acts of kindness' family. We do them because we love, not fundamentally for any expectation of return.

Let's suggest that a husband comes home and as he changes he finds a large basket of ironing on top of the washing machine, as he is about to put some dirty laundry away ready for washing. He knows his wife won't be back home for an hour and a half, will have to get dinner and everybody has to be ready to be out of the house by 7.00pm.

So out comes the ironing board and in fifty minutes he has demolished the ironing basket's contents. It's all done, well ironed and hung up in everybody's cupboard. He sits down to read the paper with a smug grin on his face. He leaves the iron upright cooling in the empty basket as a hint. Men love to hint they're being co-operative and helping. When his wife comes home, he doesn't mention the ironing and she doesn't notice till she herself takes a trip into the laundry with dirty washing.

The little squeal of delight, with a wonderful kiss, and: "Thank you darling," is the pleasure end of the business end of making a self-sacrificing decision about commitments.

I help out with the ironing on occasions at home. I see nothing unmanly about it. However, I remember the excited response from Pauline when I once hid a block of chocolate halfway down the ironing pile. I affixed a note on the chocolate that said: 'Thank you for doing all the mundane jobs so necessary to keep a home going.' However, I need to point out Pauline constantly reminds me (or is it hints) that I haven't done it for a long time.

That's the very point. There are so many mundane jobs around the home. Nobody told us about these. They are the 'business' end of the relationship. With real resolve and a conscious commitment we can turn them into the pleasure expression of who we are as a couple.

One interesting study, often touted by those in family therapy, showed that women still do three times as much cooking and food preparation than men, and also four times as much housework as men. The study further found that on average women attend to eight times as much laundry as men. Which, I think only proves one thing. Men would rather eat than have clean socks.

Current OECD Research[29] showed Australian women are doing on average just over five hours unpaid work every day, compared to well less than three for men. Compare the statistics for both men and women in respect to various 'life tasks' from the OECD research. It still shows women carry the heavier burden.

Figure 2.
Comparison Of Men & Women's Unpaid Work Time
Expenditure At Home (Australia)

Tasks Per Day	Woman's Expenditure	Men's Expenditure
Total Unpaid Work	**311 Minutes**	**172 Minutes**
1. Routine Housework	168 Minutes	93 Minutes
2. Shopping	36 Minutes	22 Minutes
3. Care For Residents	64 Minutes	27 Minutes
4. Volunteering	8 Minutes	4 Minutes
5. Travel For Family	35 Minutes	26 Minutes

29   Reported in Sydney Daily Telegraph Friday March 7th, 2014. pp.6.

The OECD Study showed because of unpaid work Australian women do not have as much leisure time as their 'sisters' in other countries. They spend up to one hour less than women in the UK playing sport, reading or watching television.

However there is hope. One recent survey released by the Council for Contemporary Families found that men's contribution in the home had increased almost threefold in the last four decades.[30]

Listen to another modern researcher: "While the number of 'house husbands' has trebled in the last 15 years, the study estimates there are still only 62,000 men in Britain who are economically inactive and say that they solely care for their family or their homes. Eight out of ten married women are said to do 7 or more hours of housework a week - the equivalent of an entire working day. Almost a third (30 per cent) do between 7 and 12 hours while 45 per cent do at least 13 hours. Just 3 per cent of married women, meanwhile, spend less than 3 hours a week on tasks around the home. The survey found that only 13 per cent of married women said their husbands did more housework than they.[31]"

In Australia, a recent report[32] indicated: "One in four dual-income households now have a woman as the main breadwinner." We should all be concerned about finding creative ways to both live sensibly, no matter whom the principle income earner is, and share the workload together whilst keeping harmony in our relationship.

It is both Pauline, and my conviction that there are no fixed roles around the house. We believe that job distribution remains fluid. Certainly, if you have a really steep driveway then you might decide that the husband puts the wheel-based garbage bin out for collection, because of the heavy weight of the weekly garbage. Maybe the lady of the home loves cooking, and so a couple decide she will do most of it. Nothing is set in concrete.

---

30 My Family Life online service - http://www.familylife.com under heading: "Who Does The Housework" by Dave Bohemia. 2008.

31 The Telegraph (UK). Research article by Patrick Hennessey. March 31st, 2013.

32 https://www.amp.com.au AMP/NATSEM Income and Wealth Report No. 34. Reported on also in The Telegraph (Sydney) Wednesday. Oct. 23rd, 2013, page 17.

Positively when the children are small, it is really important to share the load. In certain times – eg: when the lady of the home is not working and home minding children, or as another illustration sickness pervades the wife, then the majority of household jobs get predominantly done by who is 'more available.' Job distribution shifts with time-availability in various situations. Love is more than an emotion. Loving is also a practical everyday partnership in every arena of married life.

Have you heard of the amorous husband who said to his wife: "Can we try a new position tonight," with his mind clearly on the bedroom. "Yes," his wife said, "You can go behind the ironing board, and I'll lie on the lounge." Classic! So often true. Literally the most loving thing some men might do for their dear lady at night is to help.

There will be times when you're both at work, and it is a matter of all hands on deck when you get home. Come on; get the business done, and then you can get to the pleasure. Working together gives good chance to catch up, to talk, and to listen.

Listen guys it's not really fair if you come home after a day at work and veg out with the newspaper in your favourite lounge chair watching the sport. Meanwhile your beloved, who has also had a full day at work, comes home to prepare the evening meal, clean up, wash up, then do the housework till late, that another lady home all day has finished by dinner time (not that we are suggesting this female workload is right, fair, appropriate or just).

Then, your lady of the home sits down on the lounge exhausted at 10.20pm, as you look across with that little twinkle in your eye, with sex on the brain. Give it a miss. She's not in the mood or about to go anywhere. Yet, if both got into the 'chores,' the 'business' end of our real commitment to each other, then co-operative helping not only brings its own pleasure, but also possibly opens the door for pleasure.

Beverly as an airhostess can be away up to three days at a time with the longer overseas trips. Ted on the other hand has a regular nine to five job as a car salesman. Though his work involves one weekend a month, generally his weekends are free.

Nothing aggravates Beverly more than to come home to a bed unmade and dishes in the sink. We won't discuss what the lounge or dining rooms looks like. You think Ted would get the point after several intense arguments. Then, off Ted goes to the shed to work on his boat, annoyed with Beverly. As if that's evidencing maturity.

Ted and Beverly eventually sit down with a friend who is a minister. She is very helpful and helps Ted redefine his priorities to helping at home. "After all Ted, that's what Beverly's been saying. You really should try to listen to what she's really saying, not just her words."

They both went home to try. Their decision worked for a while. Beverly also found time to venture into the shed and help Ted with his boat. They spent a wondrous Saturday afternoon sandpapering and painting part of the boat together, talking, enjoying a coffee sitting in the boat. They had a sump-tuous candlelight dinner that night. Sex that evening was 'fantastic,' as Ted put it.

Sadly however, Ted and Beverly hadn't permanently moved from trying to solve last week's hurts to understanding the impact of making a commitment to be supportive of each other's roles and their co-operative function in the home. Both Ted and Beverley 'deferred' their decision-making to change the relationship for better. "We'll get round to it," never seems to quite realise its goal.

Unfortunately, after a month they were back to their old habits. If you want your relationship to blossom make a conscious mental decision and commitment towards acts of devoted service investing in each other. Don't defer. Further, support each other in the various roles of the home. Then, come what may, stick to it!

Bittman et al.[33] found, using ABS time-use data, that women in Australia do 90% of the child-care and 70% of all family oriented work. Men are get-ting better at sharing the load, but guys; we could be a 'lot' better!

---

33 Managing Work And Family. Michael Bittman, Lyn Craig et al. Social Policy Research Centre, University Of New South Wales, May 2008.

Couples are today seriously concerned about the work-related stresses of life. In the UK[34] it was found 35% of British employees would like a compressed working week (i.e. working just 4 days, even if it meant slightly longer hours in those four days). 33% would like to work from home if possible. Of part-time workers, 55% said they didn't want a full-time job.

All this comes down to the fact that deep down people believe family is important. They want to spend more time together as a family. The only thing is many individuals would have to relearn how to develop engaging behaviours in spending meaningful time as a couple or a family.

In the USA, only 11% of workers even have access to child-care and only 50% can take time off when the child is ill. The average Australian worker hasn't got a clue how privileged they are.

21stC pressures are getting to us. Let us find creative ways of solving how we work, relax, and relate.

---

34 Flexible Working Provision And Uptake, Chartered Institute of Personnel and Development, London Survey Report, May 2012.

Six

People In Glass Houses Shouldn't Throw Stones.

Actually, people shouldn't throw stones at all. Some aspects of our relationships are crafted in beautiful crystal glass of rare beauty, but you can't build your entire relationship that way. There has to be a balance of all the elements you use in the construction of your special partnership.

Throwing things at one another is definitely not the best way to enhance a relationship. Many of us grow up sometimes only exposed to poor role models. Clyde had grown up in a home where shouting and yelling were a normal part of life. Very few physical things were thrown, but words were. And words can deeply damage.

Clyde only survived and made his point by appearing aggressively loud. This is all he had seen growing up. In his home, when someone backed down the other person or family member actually moved in physically and kept the loud talking up to finalise their point. Rarely did anyone back down. No one minded. That was the done thing in their home. Strangely, there are houses like that.

On the other hand, Chris had sadly grown up in an abusive home where Dad was more drunk than sober. Every time he began to raise his voice in a drunken stupor everyone scattered, hid, and found something to do to get away.

So Clyde has learnt to move in on a person and raises his voice to get what he wanted. Chris had learnt not to say anything and 'hide' when voices were raised. Great combination I don't think. Though they were purposefully working on the fun and spontaneity side of their relationship, dealing with differences was difficult.

One day Chris saw the whole process unfold as they were together at Clyde's parent's house. The usual arguments, though the family always called them discussions, started. Chris sat right away from the action, sitting on the couch in the corner of the family room, legs drawn up under her chin, arms holding them tight.

Meanwhile Clyde's family raged. Each person was moving in on each other physically and verbally. Chris seemed like an insignificant bystander observing from afar. Then an observation hit her as to what was happening. Quickly Chris jumped up and grabbed Clyde's hand.

"Come on honey. We've got to go." Chris almost dragged Clyde out of the house. Taking the car keys she drove without saying a word for nearly five minutes. Clyde sat there speechless.

"Let's pull off and get a coffee honey," Chris said as she pulled into a huge gardening centre with an attractive outdoor eating area.

"But, we could have had one at Mums. What's up anyway?" By this time they were out of the car, walking towards the café in beautiful warm spring sunshine.

"I've just seen our problem honey. No, I'm not going to get negative or critical, but do you see what happens at your place?"

As they sipped coffee and slowly ate their delicious cream-topped carrot cake they discussed how each responded to criticism, how each handled opposition, anger and loud voices. Clyde readily admitted that very little of the criticism in his home was constructive, and he tended to duplicate the same with Chris. Chris indicated how she always withdrew when Clyde raised his voice, criticised or got angry.

"Yea, you're right. I even noticed how you were sitting at Mums today. Sorry honey. I really didn't realise what affect the 'way' I was responding was having on our marriage. Sadly I was really innocently duplicating your Dad's abusive loud behaviour when he got drunk."

"No problem," Chris offered. Such a comment calmed Clyde. "I've also just seen how I respond inappropriately, and improperly but more importantly why I respond that way," Chris offered.

Sitting there that day they put in some guidelines of how to handle criticism and anger when differences surfaced in their own relationship. Chris had noted that she always at home sat down in the padded comfortable chair in the corner of the kitchen, when Clyde got verbally loud. Clyde admitted he always stood up and walked around, arms waving, voice modulation getting louder.

"Let's make the round kitchen table in the middle of the room neutral ground. It's clearly in the centre of the room. So, whenever we have to get something off our chests, so to speak, then we both have to sit there together and talk. This way you've got to come out of the 'silent' corner and contribute. I; however, have got to stop raving, sit down and talk in a sensible tone of voice." Clyde was pleased with his suggestion, and Chris could see neither of them had an advantage in the agreement whilst both had made concessions.

Destructive criticism started to slip out of their interactions. Clyde made himself hold Chris' hand while they sat at their round kitchen table and talked. Chris didn't mind constructive criticism as long as the criticism was fair and in a modulated voice. Clyde made tremendous steps forward in how he handled his negative emotions. Chris also came out of her shell to contribute more constructively.

The round table in the middle of the room became their decision-making commitment. They called the table their 'Round Table,' because nobody was king, queen or knight, they were just equals. Nobody had the 'important' chair or position. Swords were stood aside, and nobody got cut down.

Eventually, the 'Round Table' became humorously personal as Chris would call Clyde her King Arthur and he called her his Guinevere. Once someone asked them what that meant. They smiled at each other. It was their secret.

Some years later Clyde bought a beautiful, very expensive fine china porcelain figurine of Arthur and Guinevere, as a present for Chris. The figurine now held pride of place in the centre of the round kitchen table. People who visited would often attempt to move the ornament aside to set coffee cups out, or lunch, but both Chris and Clyde would deliberately and politely move it back into the centre of the table.

Within the USA researchers conducted exhaustive studies on just over 2,000 couples[35] whose relationships were either seemingly nearly over, with

---

35 Dr John Gottman research out of The Gottman Institute. Referred to by various research units and widely quoted in family therapy journals.

talk of separation, or were in serious trouble. Each couple participated in both a series of tests and exhaustive interviews. Of interest, the following four things were present in the couples. Each couple evidenced:

- *Firstly, they showed: 'Contempt For Partner.'*

- *Secondly, they used: 'Destructive Criticism.'*

- *Thirdly, they evidenced: 'Defensiveness.'*

- *Fourthly, they exhibited: 'Stonewalling With Silence.'*

Nearly all of the 2,000 couples were shown not to use the term 'we,' with them usually adopting very independent lifestyles. Over a few weeks period the researchers gave them extensive and constructive tools to manage anger, use criticism constructively, relate without inferred double meanings, effective positive communication techniques, and the like.

The turnaround was amazing. I remember watching a film about this research, remembering initially seeing one couple sitting at opposite ends of their lounge, arms folded as if they were annoyed, knees pointing away from each other in hostile body language in their first interview. Voice tone was tense, seemingly intolerant of their spouse.

Interestingly, most couples used their spare time in isolation. They spent little to no time doing things together as a couple. The men took their boys to baseball or some other male sport or interest, whilst the women took their daughters to ballet or other female interests or sport.

As a couple they generally did little or nothing together as a family. The counselling team working with the couples helped them reorganise their schedules to do family things together. Here was the big discovery – when they were doing things together as a family, they were also doing enjoyable things together as a couple.

Several weeks later they were again filmed. Sitting on the same lounge the original couple I observed were now together up one end. Knees pointing to each other, her hand softly on his leg, and gentleness in their voices all showed vast improvement. Their statements showed they had really grasped a hold of constructive criticism and positive anger management. "We know we have a long way to go but we're…" So positive.

No longer was there the accusative 'you.' The corporate 'we' was being used.

In fact, researchers studying married couples at the University of Washington[36] could predict with 91% accuracy whether a couple would stay together or divorce, primarily by analysing the couple's initial reactions and communication patterns during disagreements.

We have to rethink criticism. Pay little attention to severely critical people. There has never been a statue erected in honour of a critic. Some people will even try to put your enthusiasm down by criticism. Don't let them.

A woman turned to a relative and said: "My husband's crazy about me." The cynic of the relative just looked up and replied: "Don't take too much credit to yourself. He was crazy before he ever met you."

At times, you just have to let the cynical remark of destructive criticism run off you like water off a duck's back. Nonetheless discern the difference and learn from the issues raised in constructive and destructive criticism.

Ask yourself what is the real key? Commitment and a firm resolve to deal with our responses; instead of our spouse's response is paramount – Confrontational Marriage! As our friend Isaac Newton found out through the wisdom of Andrew – you have to outrun the 'bulls.'

Testing times will come in all of our relationships. Rise up and form a solid, immoveable commitment to manage anger and be constructive in criticism. By so doing we will build a better person in our partner. We will produce the Beauty not the Beast.

---

36 University Of Washington Research and Gottman Institute research, Seattle, sourced from the online Wellness Library, as well as TV documentary.

Seven

ROLLING STONES GATHER NO MOSS.

The danger in some relationships is that they do settle down and fossilise. They don't move on. They turn into average, boring, moss-covered, mouldy marriages. The adage above does have some merit. To a certain extent, we have to move on or else the sheer weight of the movement of time will crush us in the abysmal dump of yesterday's ideas.

When I was at our printers one day, I noticed the following narration on his wall, by the famous, oft-referred author 'Anon.' He kindly gave me a copy. May the poem inspire you never to have an average day. Above all else, 'never' have an average relationship – never!

"This is the beginning of a New Day.
God has given me this day to use, as I will.
I can waste it, or I can use it for good.
But, what I do today is important because I am
exchanging a day of my life for it.
When tomorrow comes, this day will be gone forever,
leaving in its place something I have traded for it.
I want it to be gain, not loss, good, not evil, success and
not failure, in order that I shall not regret the price I
paid for it." *[Anon]*

Amar and Mia had been getting along really well. They had definitely turned around the passionate, desiring side of their life. Spending constructive time together was now part of their joyful daily routine. Emotionally they both felt the relationship had improved.

One weekend Amar took Mia away. She couldn't believe it. After the death of his wife, Alec, Amar's boss had lost interest in his clothing business. This was the break Amar had been waiting for. With a passion to always own their own clothes store his and Mia's dream was realised as they purchased the business.

With a business flare that seems somehow mysteriously to pervade the Indian culture, Amar doubled the sales figures in three months. Staff, profits and shop size was doubled again in twelve months. Amar worked hard, but he knew his preoccupation with the business was not helping the rebuilding of his marriage.

Mia had nothing but pride for Amar's takeover of the business and building of its potential. She was so proud of her husband's achievements. Amar's working day was occasionally longer than Mia was comfortable with, and generally he only took half a day off on Sunday.

That was why Mia was so surprised to go away for the whole weekend. Amar had reached some far-reaching decisions that he needed to discuss with Mia. "It's just over a year now since we took the business over. Things are going very well, and you have been more than patient, but I don't want to build the business at the expense of our marriage." Mia looked on, eyes a little misty.

"From the beginning of next month, I'm putting Ken in charge of all Saturdays and Sundays. Actually, he's covering this weekend. He'll get every Monday and Tuesday off, but more importantly I'll get every Saturday and Sunday off with you." For a while Amar seemed to be thinking out aloud, talking to the air. He looked at Mia again.

"But Amar, can we afford it?" Mia asked.

"Yes, I'm sure we can. But, there's a method in my madness. Sorry dear, I meant my decision for you." They both giggled. "In another twelve months, I want to double sales again. We're on target to do that. I won't be able to expand any further in the current shop facility, so we'll open a second shop, then a third. Hang on, I'm getting a little ahead of myself, aren't I? You see Ken is my best salesperson. So I need to train him to take over in the second shop, being in charge as store manager.

So what better way for Ken to learn than starting to be totally responsible for Saturdays and Sundays? This way he has to prove his sales organisation with staff, managerial and sales ability overall, daily procedures and customer relationship and service. He knows I'll be carefully comparing all that happens against existing Saturday, Sunday statistics.

I've discussed this with him, and he's very excited about the prospect of being manager of the new shop, if you're happy with it. Yet, the real plus is 'us.' Yes, honey we get our time back. I've worked everything out, if its ok with you, and I'll need to work back, or start early, just an extra half an hour to an hour maximum each day, and then only till I hire a part-time accountant when we purchase the second shop to run both businesses. This decision will give me every weekend totally free. If I don't make the decision now work will swallow us up, and where will we be, or our marriage, in ten years time?"

Mia was thrilled. Fully understanding that accepting the extra half hour plus each day just for the next year meant Amar was off for the whole weekend seemed a better deal than Mia could have ever hoped for. She was proud of Amar's resolve.

Amar had made a serious mental commitment. This was not based on passion or desire, but a clear understanding and consciousness that something as good as the further development of his business could eventually destroy his marriage. Seeing the difficulty of sustaining his marriage and his work Amar made a positive, pro-active decision.

"What is it the old advert says?" Amar asked Mia. "Good, better, best. We should never rest. Till, our good is better. And our better's best!"

Mia smiled. "Our business is good, it will get better, but not at the expense of the best – our marriage. Our relationship must determine our business, not the other way round," Amar said with conviction.

If we are aiming at the best we should make marriage-building a lifestyle, not a veneer. Our honesty needs to be open and transparent.

One blisteringly hot day of over forty degrees Celsius a family had six guests for Sunday dinner. They had no air-conditioning. A lazy ceiling fan turned slowly and didn't seem to help. The father asked five-year-old Jason to say grace. "But, I don't know what to say," he pleaded embarrassed, head down. Attempting a rescue Mother said: "Oh, just say what you hear me say Jason." All bowed their heads again.

Obediently Jason bowed his head and quietly said: "Oh, Lord, why did I invite these people here on such a hot day as this!"

Let genuineness be a little deeper.

We all have to prioritise our relationship. We cannot afford for our marriage to bog down gathering moss, becoming rustic and old. We need to keep loving actions moving and fresh. Balance out the demands. Make some serious commitments about what is important to you.

Some time ago I came across a survey of the workload of ministers of religion. Dr Samuel Blizzard[37] discovered that the average church minister worked 9 hours 57 minutes a day, seven days a week. That is a seventy-hour working week. What pressure that must put on their family?

Another USA survey of 5,000 ministers listed minister's primary concern: "In ministering to others we neglect our own families." Neither of these statistics indicates a healthy family-development atmosphere.

Balance and prioritisation are important. That is the key. Don't let the relationship get bogged down. Keep your relationship moving, up-to-date, contemporary, but also sensitive to what is necessary to build, not destroy the greatest asset you have – your relationship.

Amar and Mia are developing a strong mental position with their relationship. Clearly pro-active decision-making was taking place with a positive attitude. We all need to make strong decisions, based on a progressive mind-set, for the good of our marriage.

---

37 Dr Samuel Blizzard, Pennsylvania State University. Subject of the survey: The requirements of the modern ministry. Dr. Blizzard's initial study, which was originally published in 1985, has recently been revisited via additional research conducted by Dr. Sandi Brunette-Hill and Dr. Roger Finke – "A Time for Every Purpose Under Heaven: Updating and Extending Blizzard's Survey on Clergy Time Allocation" (*Review of Religious Research*, Vol. #1, pp. 48-64, 1999). Once again, an emergent pattern of pastoral frustration has surfaced about working hours and other ministerial pressures, and Dr. Blizzard's initial findings have been corroborated.

We need as couples to have a strong mental position on the importance of our marriage. Studies galore exist as to the extremely supportive factor in having a positive mental attitude to life's challenges. Though referring to medical situations, we can readily see the impact and implications in marriages, family and personal application of the principles. Here are just two illustrations. Just apply the same proactive positiveness to marriage.

Dr. Strain[38] from Mt Sinai Hospital New York reports that in one group of thirteen leukaemia patients diagnosed as having depression, twelve tragically died within one year of receiving bone marrow transplant. However, thirty-four of the eighty-seven patients who were classified as not depressed were still alive after two years.

In a further study of men who had heart attacks twenty-one of the twenty-five who were 'most pessimistic' died within eight years. Consider that only six of the twenty-five classified as positive passed away during the same time.

We humans are like icebergs. Only one-eighth is visible. Seven-eighths of us is submerged. What is going on beneath the surface is the vital issue. Let's challenge those relationship related issues below the surface. Develop a strong decision making mental position about the health of your marriage.

---

38 Dr Strain's work referred to in a Newspaper Article that didn't recognise the Journal or Research source, just cited results.

Eight

A Bird In The Hand Is Worth Two In The Bush.

I know this suggests we should appreciate what we've already got but can't we also get the two in the bush as well? Do we always only need to have the one in the hand? Why not a full gage of birds?

I want more out of life, not just the mundane 'one in the hand.'

In respect to extending that thought, let us focus on developing a total appreciation, acceptance, and understanding of that treasured one in our life. Let us always keep them as our 'essential other.' Oh how we praised and affirmed each other in courting days. Why does such often stop, in the lives of some, as couples grow older?

I try not to let any occasion go by, when Pauline steps off a dais from speaking to say: "That was fantastic. Boy you really nailed it," etc. I try not to let any meal go by, where Pauline cooks, without complimenting it. However, there is no need for praise when I'm cooking, just sympathy for those eating. Let's be grateful for any meal.

Now, you might say: "But I only got bake beans on toast, why be grateful for that?" Well, tonight up to 20% of the world will go to bed without a satisfying meal in their stomach, not having had much or any food that day. Maybe protein-boosted bake beans on toast is not a bad deal every now and again. And by the way it takes a lot of skill to open a tin of bake beans.

A grandmother was sitting talking to her sixteen year old granddaughter and some friends at her golden wedding anniversary party. The granddaughter, seeing grandad at a safe distance learned over to her grandmother and said: "Grandma, what are the keys to a good marriage?" Grandma and her friends smiled.

"Well, my love," she said, "just before your grandfather and I married I promised myself I would write a list of your grandfather's worst faults, which, for the sake of our marriage, I would forget and never mention again." Everybody smiled knowingly.

The granddaughter was not satisfied. Leaning in closer still and whispering she said: "Grandma, what was on the list?"

Grandmother looked around, still seeing her husband at a safe distance, then leant towards her granddaughter and mirrored her whispering. "Well honey, to be quite honest I became so busy on my wedding day I forgot to write the list. But, every time your grandfather did something that really annoyed me I'd say to myself: Thank goodness that was something on the list."

Here in the wisdom of the grandmother is commitment, lifelong commitment, to hang in, no matter what may come. She is appreciating the 'one in the hand' as well as those 'in the bush.'

Edna St. Vincent Millay once said: "Tis not loves going that hurt my days, but that it went in little ways." How tragic. Never let us treat our marriage so casually.

One survey examined the ongoing difficulties reported by couples whose relationship had all but broken down. The No. 1 response at 86% of all responders, separated by 50% from its closest contender, was this response: "We can't talk to each other."

Hang on, aren't these the same couples who as courting lovers, would sit and talk until the sun came up watching the crashing waves and circling birds at the beach? Yes! What's happened? They didn't make firm cognitive, mental decisions to keep such alive in their relationship.

I am what is termed a typical 'Type A' personality. I move at three hundred miles an hour; love dozens of projects on at once. I relish in deadlines, schedules, and pressure. Now, my Princess is not a 'Type A' personality. In fact, Pauline is the classic 'Type B.' She is Mrs Mellow.

Now who is right who is wrong? Neither. Well, what style is better, what is worse? Neither. Abandon better/worse, right/wrong, and replace these restrictive mind-controlling concepts with the liberating concept of 'different.' We are different. And, I need to clearly understand and appreciate Pauline's differences. Further to that, I need to articulate that understanding and appreciation in words and actions.

John and Julie have missed the boat when it comes to appreciation. Because of Julie's brilliant creative flare, she often misses some of the systematics of life. That annoys John. "Why can't Julie be just like I am?" he quietly mumbles to himself.

Julie on the other hand is just as bad. She looks for a more creative response out of John towards their relationship. She's intolerant of his analytical approach to life. When John brought flowers home last week, because Julie had pestered him for days, as he hadn't bought flowers for at least a year, it had ended in disaster.

John just stuck the pink carnations, with white baby breath surround in a vase with water and left them on the kitchen bench. Job accomplished! "That should satisfy her," he thought as he walked off to the bedroom to change clothes. His attitude was wrong.

"Oh for goodness sake," Julie said towards his back. "Don't you know how to arrange them?"

In those two short and even hostile statements she diminishes and nullifies his gift. So, she took the flowers out of the vase and spent five minutes at least rearranging them. Sure they looked much better. However, that's Julie's, not John's gifting, emphasis and talent.

Why can't they just understand and appreciate each other? Why has John's 'desire' factor turned to 'disinterest'? Further, they are both 'deferring' making positive 'decisions' to build and improve the relationship.

John later opens the fridge and yells loudly, as Julie is in the lounge room: "Where's the butter. Have you got it?"

She responds to what she feels is a stupid, loud hostile request, thinking: 'As if I'd have the butter in my hand.' "It's in the fridge," she yells.

John's getting exasperated: "Well, I can't see it."

Frustration in Julie's voice is now showing: "I just put it in there five minutes ago, halfway back on the shelf. Just look."

That last statement riles Mr Organised: "You must have put it somewhere else where the butter shouldn't go, because it's not in here. It's definitely not in here."

Julie comes into the kitchen and thrusts her arm over John's shoulder and produces the butter as if by magic. How did she do that? How do women in general do that?

John takes exception to this because Julie has another one up on him. But, he should appreciate her for what she is – a woman.

Women have two, not one (as with men) 'X' chromosomes. Among other things, this gives her greater depth of vision with a greater number and variety of cone-shaped cells in the eye that is producing and enhancing this female visual advantage.

Instead of laughing over differing strengths and appreciating each other's differences such becomes war to John and Julie. Childish counter responses dominate each of them, trying to get the verbal advantage.

John unfairly criticises Julie's backing ability in the car, when he knows perfectly well that research has shown men can 'out-back' a car 4:1 to women. British research has also shown that 71% of men can parallel park a car on the first attempt, compared to 23% of women.

But, consider for a moment that women are naturally far more intuitive than men. Not that John would admit it.

Couples with a maturing relationship understand each other's differences, not weaknesses. This sort of acceptance, appreciation, and understanding of each other is not something that is developed in the heat and passion of a moment.

Appreciating differences is a conscious decision I make. I mentally give ascent to this need to keep the relationship alive. I strive to do it, as an aspect of my will, for Pauline whenever I can.

Clearly, and tragically John and Julie are not making that cognitive choice, no matter how naturally brilliant each may be. They haven't developed positive decision-making commitment to support either each other, or the marriage relationship.

Conclusion To: Decisions And Life's Difficulties.

Every marriage, every relationship must suffer the attack of the 'bulls.' Things will come and things will go. The point is have we made a conscious commitment to keep on track, no matter what comes our way. Or, has our relationship stalled, we have deferred decision-making and, we are a prime target for the 'bull'?

The primary concept of this Section was related to choices we must make outside the passion, desire and heat of passionate love. I choose to love. That is a mental decision and a cold cognitive response, though lovingly it will be worked out through many considerate displays.

A UK survey of 739 men was asked what were the key factors in a good marriage. The responses were surprising:

- *Firstly:* **Loyalty.**

- *Secondly:* **Communication.**

- *Thirdly:* **Kindness.**

- *Fourthly:* **Sex.**

It is interesting that the passion issue (if you want to be restrictive in your thinking assigning it only as sex) was fourth, and the cognitive issue of making a conscious decision to be loyal came first.

So, certainly keep the motivational side alive with its passion, desire, fun and spontaneity. Make sure they are well and truly alive in your relationship. Then, add to that a firm mental decision-making commitment that come what may, you're there for the long haul – bulls or no bulls! Don't defer, the bull will hit you.

Section 3

DEMONSTRATION, THE ACID TEST OF A RELATIONSHIP.

A healthy relationship requires not only the passionate desire and conscious decision-making commitment of a couple, but also the constant, and we repeat constant, demonstration of that love. It is all very well, and necessary, to make a cognitive commitment to the relationship. This does not totally, or naturally, always ensure demonstration.

We need to show our love, give our love, and demonstrate our love. The ancient Greeks had several interesting words for love. One was 'Agape.' The deeper meaning of the word in essence means selfless, self-giving love of one person for another without necessarily sexual implications or inclusion. It may be best expressed as 'self-sacrificing love.' Healthy relationships give in a self-sacrificing way. In respect to marriage 'Agape' infers a couple demonstrating love to each other. They give for giving sake, not essentially to get something back.

Demonstrating our love frequently, and without expectation of return, is the acid test of our continuing devotion to our spouse. These actions become an unconscious part of our loving DNA.

Conscious choices should outwork themselves in practical ways with a firm 'determination' to develop and continue to develop a healthy relationship.

The Fourth Dimension of 'determination' is most effectively seen here. This we will amplify better in the next Section.

The deepening of intimacy requires a sustained demonstration of love. Some would say this expresses the emotional side of the relationship, where love is not merely a statement of fact at marriage, but a living, breathing feeling practically demonstrated in a thousand ways. However, are we always at the whim of our errant emotions? Can't we live with our emotions in order, projecting positivity into our relationship?

The opposite of this healthy 'demonstration' of love is of course 'denial.' Instead of demonstrating good positive emotional feelings we deny their existence and claim on our life and live in the denying world of self-indulgence.

Have you heard about the woman who kept a mysterious box high up on the top shelf of her linen cupboard? Her husband had asked what it was, shortly after they were married, but she made him promise he would never look in it, nor ever ask her about it again. After her firm insistence he agreed. Over their many years of marriage he often wondered what was in the box. But, he never looked in or enquired about it again.

On her deathbed, in her late eighties, the aged husband guardedly raised the subject of the box. She agreed that it was time he learned of its mysterious contents. He carefully got it down and took it to her. As she, in her weakened state, opened the lid it revealed two beautifully knitted teddy bears and nearly $80,000 in cash, some in old bank notes. "What are these teddy bears for?" he asked.

"Well I promised myself that every time you did something annoying I'd knit a teddy bear." His eyes went misty.

The husband was chocked with emotion. "Oh, you're so wonderful. You only found two things in me that really annoyed you." He smiled. She looked on also smiling, more grinning.

"But, where did all this money come from?" he now asked holding it up in disbelief.

"Oh, that's what I made from selling teddy bears," she said giggling.

Let's not be in denial like the wife above, doing nothing to actually address her concerns. Let's demonstrate our love one towards the other in loving openness. Keep accounts short.

Interesting studies are just coming to light on how our emotions seriously affect our relationship. It has been discovered that a gene involved in the regulation of serotonin can indicate how much our emotions can affect our relationships. Researchers at the University of California, Berkeley and Norwest University, with psychologist Robert Levenson[39] in the online journal *Emotion* comment: "With these new genetic findings, we now understand much more about what determines just how important emotions are for different people."

Specifically, the researchers found a link between relationship fulfilment and a gene variant, or 'allele,' known as 5-HTTLPR. All humans inherit a copy of this gene variant from their parents. Study participants with two short 5-HTTLPR alleles were found to be most unhappy in their marriages when there was a lot of negative emotions, such as anger and contempt, and most happy when there was positive emotion, such as humour, and affection.

5-HTTLPR polymorphism impacts human cingulate-amygdala interactions: a genetic susceptibility mechanism for depression. "Carriers of the short allele of a functional 5' promoter polymorphism of the serotonin transporter gene have increased anxiety-related temperamental traits, increased amygdala reactivity and elevated risk of depression."[40]

"In a prospective-longitudinal study of a representative birth cohort, we tested why stressful experiences lead to depression in some people but not in others. A functional polymorphism in the promoter region of the serotonin transporter (5-HT T) gene was found to moderate the influence of stressful life events on depression. Individuals with one or two copies of the short allele of the 5-HT T promoter polymorphism exhibited more depressive symptoms, diagnosable depression, and suicidal tendencies in relation to stressful life events than individuals homozygous for the long allele. This epidemiological study thus provides evidence of a gene-by-environment interaction, in which an individual's response to environmental insults is moderated by his or her genetic makeup."[41]

39 www.newscentre.berkeley.edu/2013/10/07/marriage-gene also reported by Saturday Edition of the Sydney Daily Telegraph Oct. 12th, 2013. Pg. 24.
40 http://www.nature.com/neuro/journal/v8/n6/abs/nn1463.html
41 http://www.sciencemag.org/content/301/5631/386.short

By contrast, those with one, or two long alleles were far less bothered by emotional tenor of their marriage, therefore coped better overall when pressures occurred and were more balanced emotionally. Obviously, advantaged are both spouses both with two longer alleles.

The new findings don't imply that couples with different variations, and shorter versions of 5-HTTLPR are incompatible, the researcher's note. Instead, the research suggests that those with two short alleles are likelier to still thrive in a good relationship but possibly suffer more poorly in a bad relationship. None of this however, ignores the fact that we have to own our own emotional responses and build strengths, not weaknesses – short or long alleles!

Now seeing no one quite knows or understands what a long or short 5-HTTLPR 'alleles' looks like I think I'll start a new business. I could sell packets of 'whatever' and market them as long 'alleles' that you could sprinkle on your morning cereals or toast, or mix in your juice, guaranteeing to enhance the emotional tenor of your marriage for the day. I can just see the packet: 'Super 5-HTTLPR, Guaranteed To Develop Healthy Emotional Responses.' I'll make a fortune and my placebo will work just fine if you're convinced inside is a set of long alleles.

More seriously, our emotions should bring, produce, and demonstrate love. The Western World has many stupid expressions: 'making love' being one of the most stupid. For a great percentage, the moment people hear this expression, they think of sexual intercourse, or that is the predominant connotation. However, there are thousands of ways we can 'make,' give, demonstrate, or invest love in a relationship.

In the same way you can bank money in a bank account and develop a healthy credit balance, you need to constantly bank random acts of kindness into the emotional bank account of your spouse. Hundreds of selfless acts of love, requiring nothing back, demonstrate your deepening intimacy.

Only those who have a healthy credit balance of 'love-inputs' can sustain the occasional withdrawal, when a couple need to graciously sort out a difference. Your marriage will probably not survive, or suffer badly, if there are constant withdrawals against a continuing zero balance love account.

One

An Apple A Day For Isaac Newton.

Time had elapsed since Isaac Newton had caught up with Andrew. Too much time in Isaac's estimation. He had heard that Andrew and Joan were to be married. Clutching a bouquet of fresh spring flowers, matching those in her hair Joan and Andrew had pledged their love and vows to each other in the manor's chapel on a beautiful late spring day. Their dress was simple but clean, lacking any of the wedding day trimmings of the wealthy. The wedding guests village friends.

Isaac had attended their wedding on that happy day and wished them every success. His gift was financial, and Andrew and Joan were deeply moved at the generosity of their friend. No honeymoon in those days for the working class. 'The honeymoon' as such didn't appear in UK culture till the 19thC.

Just over two years had passed since that wedding day meeting. On a trip to the manor, Isaac had chance to observe Andrew and Joan from an upstairs manor window.

"What are you watching?" Clive, the Lord of the Manor had asked as he entered the room.

"Oh, just Andrew and Joan down there. What a charming couple. Look at him, how he cares for her. Andrew seems to constantly be demonstrating his love towards her," said Isaac, letting the curtain go and turning towards his host.

"What, is that a problem for you Isaac?"

Isaac cut in quickly. "No! Absolutely not my Lord. Just the reverse. What a charming demonstration of good marital love. Not like many of the couples we know, hey?"

The Lord of the Manor didn't know whether to cough, splutter, choke, or all three. This comment was too close to the bone for him. Isaac smiled knowing his well intended, and deliberately aimed barb had embarrassed.

"Good Lord, what a statement Isaac. Surely, you don't expect a couple to go on like they were before marriage, after marriage?"

Isaac turned to the window not wanting to embarrass his host any further. "Why not my Lord, why not! Anyway excuse me a moment. I haven't seen Andrew and Joan for such a long time. I think I'll go down and catch up with them again. Back shortly to conclude our business." Leaving the room saved Lord Clive any further embarrassment.

Making his way downstairs Isaac found both Andrew and Joan enjoying their ploughman's lunch in the warm late spring sunshine. Both were sitting on separate empty ale barrels next to the old worn wooden stable doors, with the bottom half shut. Andrew's back was to the sun-drenched door, leaning on it. A black and white plough horse gently had his nose over the half door and Andrew's shoulder hoping for a crust, as he constantly nudged Andrew's head and hand.

Andrew and Joan hadn't seen Isaac approaching. As he came up behind them, through the back of the stable and the side door, Isaac observed more endearing actions one towards the other.

Their meeting was expectantly pleasant. Joan fondly kissed Isaac Newton on the cheek, and Andrew heartily shook his hand.

"Ah! I see a little one is on the way." Isaac could see Joan was showing with her first pregnancy. Both Joan and Andrew blushed, but were excited to share their joy with Isaac.

"Tell me Andrew. Nearly three years has passed since I first crowned you with the apple." Andrew laughed and playfully rubbed his head. "How come you are still showing that you're both still very much in love? I watched you both from up there a while ago, though you didn't know I was observing you. How can you maintain your 'momentum'?"

Andrew roared laughing at Isaac's use of 'momentum,' as Isaac pulled up an empty ale barrel and sat on it. Still laughing, Andrew handed him a piece of cheese and buttered bread torn from a small loaf on his plate. Isaac gratefully accepted. Joan wasn't quite sure what Isaac meant by 'momentum' and why Andrew laughed so heartily.

Moving a little closer to Joan and softly holding her hand Andrew said: "Don't worry honey. It has to do with bulls." Now, Joan was even more confused as both her husband and Isaac were loudly giggling like two school kids with a secret.

"Easy Professor," eventually offered Andrew. "For every loving thing Joan does, and she does so much, I do the same, doing something lovin in return. Simple ain't it. What's the good book say: 'What ya sow, ya reap.' If I sow loving actions I reap loving actions. If I 'choose' to be angry, which can appen to us all at times, and I foolishly respond from that perspective, guess what I get? Something less than what I'd like back again. Simple, ain't it Professor?"

Isaac again sat there stunned at such innocent wisdom. He thought to himself that in this seemingly uneducated couple was true pristine natural wisdom. Andrew had just articulated Isaac's Third Law of Motion, but in relationship terms. They shared a pleasant half an hour talking before Isaac went back to conclude his business and bid farewell to the Lord of the Manor, before making his way back to Trinity College.

As he walked Isaac thought about the wisdom of Andrew. Here was another important law of relationship. How could he best express it in relationship terms? He continued thinking about his Laws of Motion.

"Ah, yes: **For every action** [in a marriage] **there is an equal and corresponding or potentially opposite reaction** [one towards another]." [Laws Of Motion No. 3]

I will continue to recognise this as my 3rd law of motion, so as not to offend the sensibilities of the so-called gentry, talking about relationships. Why is it people feel so awkward about sharing about intimate relationships?"

When Andrew demonstrated love, Joan responded in just the same manner and vice-versa. No wonder they were so happy. Isaac Newton then thought about John and Mary, as he kicked the dry late spring dust along the forest pathway alongside the paddock next to the bull. Yes that bull.

Just off the pathway the last of the daffodils, under the beech and elm trees drooped their fading heads as fresh bluebells were springing to life everywhere in the shade. An English Wild Dogwood rose of soft white/pink flowers intertwined with the paddock's fence was beginning to blossom.

Isaac smiled when he saw what he had christened 'Bartholomew The Bull'. He was sure the bull was deliberately starring back. With his clean white face, beautiful red, brown and white hide with his authoritative stance made him look forbidding. He snorted at Isaac, as if remembering previous encounters.

Isaac thought about his college friends. How impersonal John and Mary were with each other. Often, Isaac had heard Mary's resentful comments to John, only to hear his acid tongue in return. Sadly, their children reflected the same disrespecting attitude towards each other, their parents and people in general. "Those sort of attitudes spread like the bubonic plague," Isaac muttered to himself.

Then there was Edward and Elizabeth. Pillars in the local church Isaac thought: "Just, as hard!" he said out loud. Edward continued to have the occasional affair. What a disgrace to the cause of true Christianity and marriage. Everyone, including Elizabeth, pretended they didn't know. Yet, they all did, including the area bishop. How did Elizabeth respond? She deliberately spent more money than they had. If Elizabeth couldn't have his affection, she'd have his money and spend till it hurt him. And her spending really hurt Edward.

For every hurtful action on his part there was an equal and corresponding hurtful, even spiteful action on hers. "And, they're supposed to be adults," thought Isaac.

It was common knowledge that Edward and Elizabeth had blistering arguments in their home, oblivious to who might hear. And it was easy to hear.

Then, they would come out into public as if nothing were wrong and act the model-married couple. They were denial and hypocrisy personified.

"Blasted hypocrites," Isaac mused. "Why can't people be real and genuine, just like Andrew and Joan?"

So many couples that Isaac knew had lost their passion, their genuine desire for each other. Yet, they lived ignorant in denial. This saddened him when considering the viability of marriage.

Then, so many married couples lost the resolve and decision-making commitment to make the relationship work. Finally, rarely, if ever, did they genuinely demonstrate their love.

Oh yes, they got a reaction, but their reaction was not a relationship-building response; it was relationship-destroying reaction.

The Challenge: *To deepen the intimacy in our relationship we need to constantly, actively demonstrate self-sacrificing love. We need to be pro-active, not reactive. What we sow, we will reap. Essential to a growing relationship is the giving of love, without the mandatory expectation of a return.*

Two

A Picture's Worth A Thousand Words.

A picture may be worth a thousand words, but the tenderness of a whispered "I love you," when least expected is more highly prized than a Picasso. Don't you only want someone's picture of love, or tender words and communication uplifting you? Never, ever lose the power of uplifting positive words. From coming through and maintaining the passion and desire in a relationship, we have sealed love with a conscious commitment and decision to love through the difficult times. Now comes the continuing demonstration that illustrates and evidences that growing relationship.

Positive communication must exude from every fibre of our being if we are to maintain a growing, enriched marriage. Some years ago, The Ladies Home Journal in the USA undertook an interesting survey with women. Among the questions towards the front of the survey was this paraphrased question: "Upon what basis did you originally select your partner?" The survey gave a great list of options often in typical media emotionally charged terms we may not feel expresses best opinion. The top response of the ladies was: "Sex appeal."

The survey then asked many more questions but towards the end of the survey was this interesting paraphrased evaluating question: "If you ever had to do it all over again upon what basis would you now select your partner?"

Now, the No. 1 response was: "His ability to communicate," chosen from the same provided list as the original responded to question.

They now didn't care if he looked like the back end of a bus, as long as he could communicate. What do we mean by communication? If you think just talking, or correctly more talking, then I think you have missed the point.

As a professional counsellor I can tell you that some people Pauline and I see for counselling need less communicating, if your understanding of communication is just talking. Most would say: "Surely, they need more communication?" Yet, if their only communication (on your definition of communication being verbal) is fighting, yelling, and screaming, then surely they need to do less of that destructive behaviour, not more.

Communication is far more complex, but we can all extend our understanding and grasp of it. An English teacher was trying to extend the communicative skills of his students by helping them extend their vocabulary. "I assure you," he said, "if you repeat a word ten or twelve times, it will be yours forever."

At the back of the room a stunning seventeen year old blond female student took a deep breath, closed her eyes, put her hand over her heart and whispered into the air: "Greg, Greg, Greg…" in a sultry, dreamy fashion and voice.

Communication is everything we do, inclusive of our verbal intercourse. That's why I think communication is more a catalyst to other life-skills, rather than a raw skill that sits on its own, isolated from everything else.

A wink is communication. A kiss blown across the hand is communication. A rose on her pillow is communication. An 'I love you' card sent in the mail is communication. How are you communicating?

Communication in every form should build intimacy. The emotional side of our relationship is released in a wholesome way, when the communication is itself wholesome, seeking as its primary goal to build the other person.

Here is one key to effective communication, which builds powerful self-esteem. When I know who I am, when I have dealt with the garbage of the past and am secure in my sense of worth, then the way I tend to reach out to others is to make them look good. So everything flowing from me, in how I communicate, seeks to fulfil and uplift my wife, my children and family, my grandchildren, my friends, and many others. I am totally content with building others.

What I get back in return is immense satisfaction. To see others reach their potential, and to know you have contributed is fantastic.

However, when I don't know who I am there is a problem. When, I haven't dealt with issues of the past, and within me, the way I tend to reach out to others is to attempt to make others make me look good. And, that my friend is too hard for any relationship to sustain. We generally alienate those people, and relationships consequently suffer.

Several years have elapsed since we first met Tony and Cheryl. They have rediscovered the passion and desire in their relationship and made conscious and committed decisions about where they want their relationship to go. Even their son David, now married with his first child is impressed with Dad. He can even now have a sensible conversation with Dad, without him flying off the handle.

"Don't know what you've done to Dad Mum, but it's working. Keep it up," David quipped, looking at his mother, as he went out the back door with his wife and daughter. His sister who was also leaving on her way back to university also giggled calling out: "Amen!"

Cheryl playfully grabbed David's arm and whispered: "He's done it himself son. Rather nice isn't it?"

Communication on every level now becomes a natural outflow of the desire side of their marriage, being reinforced by the decision side of their relationship. Cheryl loves Tony's little squeezes as he walks by her. She knows that doesn't need to lead anywhere, but sometimes it does, but always at her instigation. How their love life had changed. Now, it is an outflow of their relationship, not a chore to be performed occasionally.

They both have learned to listen. Their long walks on the beach with their energetic brown and white Charles Cavalier dog Buster, who loves chasing seagulls, is their favourite pastime. All such actions are communication.

Professor Albert Mehrabian[42] in the late twentieth century discovered that there were three interesting components, among others, to the way we convey any message. His research is still quoted by many today and has been reinvestigated and authenticated further by those continuing in family therapy/counselling. It has not lost its relevance.

In diagnosing communication, Mehrabian discovered that:

- *7% of the message is conveyed by the words we use.*

- *38% of the message is conveyed by the tone of our voice.*

- *The final 55% of the way we convey a message is made up from our nonverbal communication.*

We generally presume that because we spoke we have communicated. Not at all! Often, we get ourselves into trouble not because of what we've said, but how we've said it. Tony and Cheryl discovered this one Monday morning.

As Tony was reading the paper, he was checking out the weekend sports results as he finished his toast and coffee. He had missed catching up with weekend soccer matches on TV, or the radio news. Tony had to leave for work in a few minutes. He was decidedly unhappy about the fact that his favourite football team had lost so badly the previous night. "Now where will we be on the score ladder?" Tony mumbled.

Meanwhile, Cheryl sneaking up behind him put a kiss on the side of his neck and softly said: "I love you." However, Tony was still engrossed in his morning paper, sport, and the misery of his team's defeat. Head still entrenched in the paper he said: "Love you," in a loud, stern almost aggressive way. Cheryl was temporarily taken back.

Now let us for a moment examine Tony's communication contribution. What message did he really convey? First, you can't fault his words. Tony only

---

42 Primary work mid to late 1960. Mehrabian's work featured strongly mid-late 1980-90s, University of California, Los Angeles. Others have extended Mehrabian's work in more recent years.

had two – 'love you.' So far, so good. We'll give Tony 7%, or seven out of seven for that. But, what about the tone of his voice? Though his words were saying 'I love you,' his tone of voice was actually saying: 'Go away, and go away now. I'm more interested in the sports page.'

This is not good. Now, Tony has 38% backing up against him. His tone of voice was not saying: 'I love you.' Then finally, Tony wasn't even polite enough to take his head out of the paper. His nonverbal communication was negative and destructive. So another 55% is backing up against him. So in finalities 7% of his message says Tony loves her, whilst 93% is sending a message of disinterest.

Tony looks up at Cheryl who is pretending to look hurt and rubbing her eyes as if playfully crying, softly mockingly whimpering. Tony took only a fraction of a second to cotton on. "Oh, sorry darling. That was rude of me, wasn't it?" Tony grabbed her tenderly, pulling her into his lap and gave her a meaningful cuddle, and kiss with a lovely six-minute chat before leaving for work.

It is important to remember communication can be quite varied. At work early one morning, in mid February, Tony received a 'Thank You' card from his boss for a project well done. He thought about how satisfying and rewarding it was to receive it, with the associated praise from both his boss and the company, also how it made him feel valued. His brain kept on coming back to that concept throughout the day. Then he hit on an idea. He now thought of the perfect way to demonstrate his love to Cheryl for Valentine's Day next year, seeing this year's Valentine's Day had just been successfully celebrated last week.

Tony purchased a beautifully hand crafted, burgundy, and Moroccan leather-bound book with 96 blank handmade linen-paper pages in soft lilac colour. He had Cheryl's name embossed in gold on the front. Every week, in the privacy of his work office, for a whole year he would write a full page to a page and a half thank you letter to his wife, thanking her for every thing she had done that week. He itemised even small things she had done, and what she meant to him. He dated every week's entry. On Valentine's Day the following year he presented it to her beautifully boxed, tied with a gorgeous red ribbon and red rose on top, alongside a dinner reservation for that night at an exclusive city restaurant.

Cheryl was so overtaken with emotion she couldn't stop joyfully crying for an hour. The book meant more to her than all the expensive presents she had ever received. It held pride of place on her dresser in the bedroom from that day forward.

Communication is more than talking. Communication is who we are, expressing our love in a thousand creative ways.

Our communication needs to flow out of all we are. Let communication deepen intimacy. Let such express the true emotional strength that we have. Communication should be a healthy 'daily' display of our love, not a verbal minefield we have to dodge around. It should project, nurture, and convey love.

Three

If At First You Don't Succeed, Try, Try Again.

We need to clearly understand that we can succeed in small steps the first time. Success should not always be seen as a one-off event, an optimum experience, but a journey. Finding ways that don't work is not failure; it can be viewed as success of learning non-productive ways, if we truly learn from it.

A newlywed husband tried valiantly to console his bride of one month who was sprawled out on the sofa, weeping her heart out.

"Darling," he implored, "believe me, I never said you were a terrible cook. I merely was pointing out that our kitchen sink garbage disposal unit has developed a bad case of heartburn and an ulcer."

I think he should find another approach to raising issues he wants to talk about. Remember communication and life is a learning curve.

They tell us Edison only went to school for three months of his life (but keep in mind urban myths abound). His Mother is said to have educated Thomas at home. Yet, he is accredited with patenting around one thousand inventions just in the USA alone and over two thousand, three hundred worldwide, including the incandescent light. Edison diligently experimented for years developing the incandescent light. Many people viewed the experiments that did not work as failures.

A young reporter boldly asked Edison if he felt like a failure in an interview. Eyeballing Edison the reporter insensitively further asked if he thought he should have just given up by now. Perplexed, Edison replied, "Young man, why would I feel like a failure? And why would I ever give up? I now know definitively over 9,000 ways that an electric light bulb will not work. Success is almost in my grasp." And shortly after that, and after over 10,000 attempts, Edison invented the light bulb.

There is always a better way. A better mousetrap awaits invention. We all trust cars can eventually be made out of what they make 'black boxes' out of for aeroplanes – hopefully! In these times we live in none of us can afford to remain static in what we do and how we do it. The smart person, the true lover, will always be looking for a way to be a better man, a better woman. They will be practicing Confrontational Marriage – confronting themself continually to bring their marriage into continuous and sustained intimacy.

Do we have the same way today of looking at our marriage, as years ago? Are we smart enough to see ways and attitudes that don't work and therefore we're intelligent enough not to go down that path again? Are we in love enough to look for a better way that works? Do we crave intimacy so dearly as to find what produces the Beauty and not the Beast?

In the United Kingdom 32% of all divorces now occur after the age of forty-five, compared to 23% ten years ago.[43] Are we getting less patient, less tolerant of each other? Sounds like the 'Beast' has been awakened.

Sadly John and Julie are bringing out the Beast in each other. Wouldn't you think, as intelligent, well-educated people, they would be smart enough to see that whenever something hurt their spouse they then should be sensitive enough, even intelligent enough to change it? Tragically no, they won't budge an inch.

Dreams are long gone. I'll guarantee they could hardly tell you what their original dreams had ever been. This deterioration of their marriage hasn't just begun today; this decay is the result of years of neglect, indolence, and pride – stinking, human pride. Why do we humans find it so hard to admit we're wrong? Why won't we change?

---

43   David Fletcher; Health Service Correspondent; The Daily Telegraph (UK), March 20, 1996.

John and Julie have replaced 'things' for their goals. Whereas intimacy should be to each of them an ultimate goal, now they have 'things,' and 'things' have them. Neither of them is truly happy.

Their determination is not to find intimacy, though John has his own ideas on what the term 'intimacy' means. Their driving goal is to survive without being hurt and to keep the upper hand. It dominates John and Julie's thinking. Oh, they have discovered the emotional side of their relationship all right – just the bad emotions.

Shouting or silence seems to be their two favourite ways of verbally interacting. But, you could hardly call either effective communication, displaying mature emotional well being.

John has met Sandra at work, another senior executive. She seems to lift him up with her words. The way Sandra touches his hand when she hands him some paper work, or deliberately rests a hand on his shoulder as she leans over from behind discussing the contract on the table, sends a thrill through his body. Now there's a determination in John. Keeping his new love interest a deadly secret from what he calls 'Attila The Hun' back home is John's driving motivation.

Finding a better way to communicate and improve the marriage is not high on John or Julie's agenda. John's business trip away is totally ignored by Julie. She doesn't care where John goes or for how long and what purpose.

Sandra does! She makes sure she is on that same trip. So begins the affair with the same passion and desire originally John and Julie once had for each other.

John and Julie could have kept their passion alive and renewed their desire. They could have, with steely determination, made decisions of commitment to face life's obstacles with a view of conquering them together. They could have risen in intimacy that flowed from a safe and warm emotional response to each other.

They could have. But, they didn't. Did you know happiness has a reset button? Push it! Sadly John and Julie's are not even looking, or interested in looking for their reset button. 'Demonstration' of love tragically gives way to 'denial.' They are not only denying each other's needs; they are denying their own.

Now, we have John in an affair, and Julie off shopping again.

Research into longevity in marriage has been widespread. Markham, Stanley and Blumberg[44] (PREP, University of Denver), as well as Threshold Journal in Australia have identified the well-known principle that often couples stay together whilst the children are the focus of the relationship.

When the children leave the home, tragically for some so does the reason for staying together. In the USA between 1981 and 1991 divorce dropped by 1.4%, whilst divorce among those married thirty years or longer increased 16%.

UK daily press[45] reported on what is being termed: 'The Silver Divorce' – couples divorcing after 25 years of marriage. In 1993, there were 1,500 such divorces in the UK that year. By 2005 it had risen to 3,000. Now 'Silver Divorce' accounts for over 16% of all UK divorces.

Markham et al. research showed that the greatest indicator of a healthy long-term marriage was 'having a strong couple-friendship.' Though the definitive understanding of what is meant by that phrase may vary slightly, we get the overall point.

Sadly John and Julie haven't heard about this 'couple-friendship.' Or, they choose to ignore it. Clearly they are not 'demonstrating' love towards each other. They have tragically replaced that 'D' with another couple of their own 'Ds.' 'Defensiveness' and 'denial' now dominates the way they respond to each other. Desire has gone, and their decision making process is on hold when it comes to good healthy marriage-building decisions.

Sadly healthy, loving demonstration of love has now been slowly turned into denial of each other's needs and replaced by arrogant defensiveness.

John and Julie are on a slippery slope downwards. They never think of doing 'nice' things for each other. Selfless acts of loving, requiring nothing in

---

44 Fighting for Your Marriage: Positive Steps for Preventing Divorce and Preserving a Lasting Love. Markham, Stanley and Blumberg [University of Denver], Pub: Josses-Bass, 2001, cited by Threshold Journal [Australia].
45 Daily Telegraph (UK) nd.

return, is like a foreign language – they cannot speak its beauty in their life. They have an unhealthy balance of 'hurtful' actions to 'healing' actions.

The Journal of Personality and Social Psychology[46] examining the research of John Gottman and Robert Levenson showed that successful marriages have a 5:1 or better ratio of good behaviours to bad marital experiences. So, we need to ask ourself: "For every one bad experience, when we upset our spouse, knowingly or unknowingly, are we offering more than five wonderful self-sacrificing, random acts of kindness?"

If so our marriage will probably succeed. If the ratio is lower than 5:1 (Caring actions = 5; Hurtful actions or experiences = 1), then research indicates we may be headed for matrimonial trouble, even divorce.

Tough research. But it capably illustrates our need to constantly be 'demonstrating' our love, so when there is an accidental misunderstanding, there has been a better than five positive contributions to cushion the one difficult time.

Keep in mind however, that 5:1 is the minimum ratio or satisfactory pattern stated as required. We should personally be aiming at a significantly higher ratio for our own personal satisfaction and the wellbeing of our marriage such as 20: 1; 30:1 or whatever. Or, let us be challenged to totally and completely eradicate the one disappointing experience.

---

46 Journal of Personality and Social Psychology, 1992, Vol. 63. No. 2. pp. 221-233 Article on 'Interpersonal Relations and Group Process' from the research article of John Gottman and Robert Levenson entitled: 'Marital Processes Predictive of Later Dissolution: Behaviour, Physiology, And Health.'

Four

LET BYGONES, BE BYGONES.

I truly believe we have to let the past go. Being shackled to past mistakes and continually being reminded of them is tantamount to having a wound that is healing and we keep taking the bandage or sticking plaster off, poke the wound, opening the sore up afresh with all its pain, just to bandage, or cover it up again and repeat the whole sorry process some days later. The wound will never heal.

However, having said that, you can't just ignore issues from the past. There must be a point where you deal with them properly, forgive if necessary, repair, and restore where appropriate and move on. However, people deal with their hurts in such a wide variety of ways.

A small six-year old boy suddenly slipped, falling badly on the floor of his classroom. His teacher hurried to console him. "Remember Jeremy, big boys don't cry." But keep in mind that is totally untrue.

"I'm not going to cry," snapped back Jeremy, "I'm going to sue."

True intimacy knows something about the past and doesn't let such issues affect the relationship negatively because the foundation between the couple is forgiveness. Somehow forgiveness seems to grease the axil of life and allows us to move on.

Chris and Clyde have moved back to being deeply in love since we met them first. They have rekindled passion and made a conscious decision to interact positively when difficulties arise in a sensible, sane, and relationship-building manner. Little things still come up that irritate either or both of them. They have come to notice that when they avoid the 'Round Table' that they reverted back to old habits.

Understanding how easily they slipped back into old ways of handling issues they discussed their mutual concern and observation over coffee and croissants one Sunday morning. You guessed it; they made the 'Round Table' their venue.

"Honey, notice the other day when we were differing over what car to buy, you were at the table here, but I was still standing," Clyde offered gently patting Chris' hand.

"Yes, and you were definitely loud. I was wandering where our discussion would end up," Chris offered looking to see what kind of response she would get.

"I know. It seems that my little Guinevere is a lot smarter than Arthur," Clyde said lightening the atmosphere as they both laughed.

Clyde grabbed a book he had just purchased. "Listen to this section on habit formation." He then went on to read a section that indicated that any habit, whether a good one, or a bad one, takes from thirty to sixty days to form.

"I'll bet that's why most diets crash," said Chris.

"Exactly," butted in Clyde. "They don't last the thirty to sixty days to form a new eating regime. However, I was more thinking about 'us' things. Well, you know my old habit was to stand, to yell, to be loud and to move in on someone."

Chris thought she would chip in, but thought better of it. She just smiled knowing how negative their clashes had been in the past.

Clyde cut into her thoughts: "Well, I'm pretty impressed that both of us have come out of our corners, so to speak, and have found middle ground. In effect, what we're doing is creating our own culture. Your family culture taught you to withdraw. Mine taught me to be loud and advance aggressively."

"And be obnoxious," Chris added cautiously, but smiling. Clyde laughed. Chris joined in knowing there was no way he would have taken a comment like that a few years ago.

"But here," Clyde said, knocking the table, "is our culture. Not mine, not yours, but ours. Here is where we've worked something out."

"Yea, and it's good," added Chris, "but it doesn't always work a hundred per cent of the time."

"No, that's right honey. Notice when one of us leaves here we revert back. Look at this." Clyde was thumbing through his book. "Here is a chapter headed: 'Eight Steps Forward, Two Back.' It says often in forming new and better habits we move eight steps forward so to speak, but then unintentionally, often innocently, slip two steps back, heading back into old habits because we're so used to them."

Chris was slowly sipping her hazelnut-flavoured coffee as wisps of steam lazily drifted upwards. "But, by very definition we've still making six steps forward or ahead aren't we?" she offered.

"Exactly honey. That's my point and the point of this chapter. Progress is progress. Sure I'd rather take eight steps forward and stay eight steps forward, not slipping back two steps. Yet, six steps forward is much better than none, and the relationship is not going backwards. The chapter then goes on to say we should then positively deal with what caused the two steps backwards and apologise.

Then, we move forward again. Maybe this time nine steps forward, then possibly only one or half a step back. We need to keep working on it. I'm sure you've got the point. And 'Apology Becomes Our Friend' is another good chapter here. Great concept," said Clyde handing the book to Chris open at that chapter.

Chris shared, as she glanced at the pages, how that she felt much safer emotionally at the table, and that a more relaxed feeling overall was spreading into all the relationship.

"We're deepening intimacy," Chris said as Clyde quickly flicked his eyebrows up and down at the word 'intimacy.' She playfully slapped his arm. "That too!" Chris commented.

"Yes, I get the point honey. Here, we are developing our culture," said Clyde as he tapped the table. "Here we do not have to be like either of our parents, or our old homes. We're finding what works for us. Rekindling our desire, passion, and romance have triggered a firm commitment and decision to build our relationship come what may. Now, we see that demonstrated in the power of forgiveness as we both are positively changing our behaviours to more proactive, relationship-building behaviours."

Clyde lifted his croissant and almost took it in one bite.

"I thought it was hilarious the other day," offered Chris, "when we were at your parent's house. There, they were in full flight discussing something at the top of their voices, each trying to win a point, physically moving in on each other. Interestingly, you were sitting with me on the deckchair swing, chatting almost oblivious to it all."

"Oh, I wasn't oblivious. With that noise you couldn't be. It's just I was determined not to slip back to old habits. I know what I like. I know what works for us. Though it took everything in me to sit still, I was wanting to 'demonstrate' my commitment at that time."

Changing behaviours is not always easy. Change does not come easily or speedily to any of us. So be patient with yourself and with your partner as you specifically target issues. I find a good way to continue to keep the issue you're dealing with before your attention, is to literally keep the commitment written down before your eyes. What do I mean?

Let us consider as a husband you're trying to develop the skill of being a better listener. Then write yourself a note. Stick your note up next your ties you may wear daily, or on the bedroom mirror, or in your diary – anywhere you will continually see it. You need to remind yourself. You need to keep your goal in front of your eyes and your mind. I work on the following principle, and it has nothing to do with age, just our humanity - 'My 'forgettery' works much better than my memory.' So remind yourself.

Deepening intimacy will see us willingly but slowly changing our behaviour and lubricating the axils of that process with buckets of the oil of forgiveness. In reality, we are demonstrating love.

Wolcott, Glezer and Harris[47] have identified contemporary expectations in marriage. Today there is a high value placed on meeting each other's emotional, sexual, and companionship needs. This is a more daunting task,

---

47 Cited in: Review Of The Literature: Strong Families And Satisfying Marriages, Australian Institute Of Family Studies, Family Matters, No. 53, Winter 1999.

perhaps, than fulfilling the more clearly defined, older-view 'provider father' and 'housewife mother' role of more traditional times. The new demands are where 'intimacy' is put under the microscope and often comes up wanting.

To some extent, the traditional marriage with its focus on adequate performance of sex-oriented roles has been superseded by the concept of the 'companionate marriage', which emphasises the quality of the relational aspects more than the instrumental performance of roles. Current studies on divorce back this up when they cite common reasons or causative factors of divorce as loss of affection, an absence of caring, lack of communication and growing apart before any idea of not fulfilling a 'role.'

Hartin[48] suggests: "Whereas formerly marriages were held together by external pressures, economic necessity, and fear of social disapproval, now marriages stand or fall according to the strength of the emotional bonds between the partners."

One website encouraging emotional awareness and openness suggests: Emotional intimacy is developed through each spouse's ability to be totally open about how he or she is feeling and what they want in the relationship. If you or your spouse are shut down and find it difficult to share it can have a detrimental effect on your relationship. From the context of marriage, such emotional intimacy is a psychological event that occurs when the trust level and communication between spouses is such that it fosters the mutual sharing of each other's innermost selves. It is uninhibited mutual self-disclosure.

Sadly, a lacking of emotional intimacy in relationships is common, and as a result we pay a heavy a price. Its absence can easily be witnessed by way of strained and failed relationships of those all around us, and in a larger context, reflected within the deteriorating attitude to stable and long-term marriage commitment.

Sobering words. Emotions matter. Are we building our partner, or our role through positive emotions?

---

48   Ibid: Hartin (1988: 10).

Five

PRACTICE WHAT YOU PREACH.

Ted and Beverly didn't practise, but oh, how they would preach. They would lecture each other on: "If only you would…," but hardly ever did it themselves.

We shouldn't 'preach' in a relationship. Each of us has a vulnerable ego, delicate emotions, sensitive heart and an easily wounded human spirit. We don't often take kindly to the bruising that 'preaching' brings. We don't appreciate pontificating pronouncements of expertise from someone we know isn't doing everything they could themself.

When true passionate desire and romance continue in a couple, they learn to practice not preach. Developing a conscious commitment helps the relationship come through to a deepening intimacy that openly manifests, among other things, honesty and integrity.

Look at couples that have pushed through to develop a wonderful life together. A natural outflow of their hearts is honesty with each other and integrity. Without these two qualities, the relationship will flounder. And, it seems, you can't work them up at earlier stages in the relationship. They must grow, or prove themselves naturally. Positively, you can make a conscious decision about them in the decision-making, commitment phase that is dealt within Section 2. Generally; however, they have to flow out of the essence of who we become together.

Because a relationship rises to a certain level, a couple's intimacy facilitates them being totally honest and only responding with integrity with each other. We are not hiding; we are openly vulnerable to our beloved. They really know us. It's not so much that we have to specifically work on it. Honesty just flows out.

Sadly, Ted and Beverly's marriage is not working. They are not being honest with themselves and certainly not being honest with each other. Beverly's work schedule now deliberately is totally consumed by overseas flights. This is taking her away from home nearly four days out of every seven. Beverly especially applied for the position, though she told Ted: "We don't get any say. It's either take it or they find someone else for my job. What could I do?"

When we start continually lying to our spouse we need to realise our relationship is in serious trouble. Lying as a lifestyle leads to ruined relationships at every level.

Ted is unhappy, but Beverly doesn't care. She stopped caring a long time ago about his happiness, only her own. She has no intention of pressing the happiness-reset button. Her overseas trips bring her in contact with other maritally disgruntled aircrew that is also using their absence from home for the same reasons.

For Beverly and Ted, frequent 'demonstration' of their love to each other stopped ages ago. 'Denial' of their responsibility to fulfil their spouse and to meet their needs socially, emotionally, intellectually, and physically tragically consumes their actions. Self-sacrificing love is no longer important.

Beverly begins flirting and responding to flirting that she would have been repulsed by in their early years of marriage. She abandons her expectation of herself in the social integrity areas. Though Beverly is not in any affair at this stage, she is dangerously close to it.

What both Ted and Beverly are demonstrating is marriage-destroying behaviour.

As much as Beverly tries to convince herself: 'everybody is doing it,' Beverly knows she has to make choices. The work place is an environment where we need constantly to live with the 'integrity sensor' on full alert. We should have the common sense to know that integrity holds a great relationship together.

Alison Konrad and Barbara Gutek[49], Professors of Psychology at Claremont Graduate School says: "Sex is a problem for one half of workers. 50% of all workers report having been associated with some form of socio-sexual experience." And, they further contend as researchers that as many as thirty-five million USA workers will have such an experience in any given week.

Beverley illustrates that when the 'integrity gate' has been left unlocked, the horse can bolt. Isn't it strange how one can apply integrity to their work, but not to their own morals or life? However, when the relationship has been positively built up, we find that integrity and honesty are key stabilising factors.

Ted wasn't doing any better either. He's already had one adulterous relationship during one of Beverly's trips away. Just a 'one-night stand,' as Ted called it. No big deal in his thinking. When Beverly comes home Ted however finds he is deliberately lying about everything about the past few days to create a smoke screen for his own conscience. Funny how lack of honesty and integrity leads to blame. "Well, if Beverly met my needs I wouldn't need to go looking elsewhere." As if that's a valid excuse.

When we build and build and further build our relationship then we wouldn't dare live out of a fundamental flawed integrity base or dishonesty. Both Ted and Beverly seem natural by-products of unhealthy relationships, when they abandoned personal integrity and honesty.

I have absolutely no tolerance for pornography. Especially and perversely pornography debases sex, healthy relationships, women and children, now even men. On more than one occasion, despite the room being 'supposedly' cleaned, I have found pornography in my hotel room left there by a previous, less than integrity-living guests. I immediately find a garbage bin outside of my room and as far away from my room as possible and dump the trash, unopened and unread. That's where it belongs – pure filth and trash.

---

49 Impact Of Work Experiences On Attitudes Towards Sexual Harassment, Barbara Gutek, Alison Konrad: Claremont Graduate School, *Administrative Science Quarterly*, 1986 Johnson Graduate School of Management, Cornell University.

I am always careful to tell Pauline about these situations. "You'll never guess what was in my hotel room in San Jose..." Now, I know I can hear some saying. "I'd never tell my spouse." Why? Only what you keep in the dark has power over you.

You see Pauline knows I only want our relationship to flow in honesty and integrity. With deepening intimacy, they occur naturally. Aim for both areas. Develop both honesty and integrity. Let them support your relationship, not threaten it.

Truth and integrity are core values of any valuable relationship, whether in marriage, business, or social. When they are violated, the relationship can quickly crumble. Yet, we live in a world of few values, and a scant regard for truth and integrity, until it suits. Most of the community lives by situational ethics yet demands absolutes of those in authority. Rather hypocritical don't you think?

In the classic book, *The Day America Told The Truth*[50] we discover that 91% of people said that they lie regularly and one third of AIDS carriers admitted to not having told their partners. The book revealed that most people 'goof' off around seven hours a week at work, and most have called in sick when they were perfectly well (great having them as staff). Only 13% of Americans see all the Ten Commandments as binding.

Within an article in The Christian Post, Jerry Newcombe cites a survey of what individuals would be prepared to do for ten million dollars.[51] Newcombe further cites Mark Koba Writing for CNBC, who penned a report, "Just the Scent of Money is Corrupting: Study," citing the work of researchers in the University of Utah and Harvard in his article. It illustrates the lack of ethics and integrity in our society.

Here are some of the answers to what people would do for ten million dollars. It reflects today's society ethic/value-base.

25% said they would abandon their church. Also 25% said they would abandon their family. 23% said they would become a prostitute for a week,

50 The Day America Told The Truth, James Patterson, Peter Kim Pub: Prentice Hall Press, 1991.

51 http://www.christianpost.com/news/what-would-you-do-for-ten-million-dollars-98400

whilst 16% said they would leave their spouse. It was also 16% who said they would give up their American citizenship. And, it is cold comfort to know that 7% said they would kill a stranger.

I highly recommend reading M. Scott Peck's *People Of The Lie*[52] (Author also of: *The Road Less Travelled*). It is deep intense reading, but well worth the effort, illuminating the association of lies and the premise of evil. Peck writes a brilliant, yet disturbing book forcing us all to confront the darker side of our nature. His work is a powerful piece of research exploring the very fundamental nature of truth in human beings as well as our relationships. Peck brilliantly challenges us about truth and its place in our life. Some of Peck's concepts are rather discomforting.

Peck says: *"Lies confuse. The evil are 'the people of the lie,' deceiving others as they also build layer upon layer of self-deception."*[53] Further, Peck talks of this lying as evil that can have a disastrous effect: *"Their 'goodness' is all on a level of pretence. It is, in effect, a lie. This is why they are the 'people of the lie.*[54] No marriage can survive with 'pretence' as an integral part of its DNA. Let us be people of truth and walk and talk truth into the lives of all around us.

The fundamental objective within this book you're now reading is we want you to apply what we have called 'Confrontational Relationships.' Again, we categorically state we are not talking about confronting our partner, but seriously confronting ourself, and further, doing something about such issues to produce a better relationship.

Deep down we have to make the changes. Deep down we know what's right. We just need the guts to own the issue and do something about it. You need to change. Leave the changes in your partner to them. Be proactive in bringing the best out of them by your confrontational approach to yourself.

Fundamentally we know what the real honesty, integrity issues are. General marriage/family research shows that 98% of couples agree that monogamy in a relationship is very important. Being sexually faithful to each other is a clear demonstration of integrity and honesty. In a '0'to '10'scale both men and

---

52 People Of The Lie, M. Scott Peck. Pub: Arrow, 1988.
53 Ibid. Pg. 74.
54 Ibid. Pg. 84.

women rated faithfulness, good communication, mutual respect, understanding and tolerance, each with a 9+ score. A happy sexual relationship was given an overall 8+, whilst sharing household chores reaches almost 8.

We need to be honest with ourself in what works and simply apply the truths we hold dear. You don't need to be dull because you're truthful. Let's illustrate.

Jasmine, an unmarried twenty-five young lady worked in a busy office. When she arrived early one morning, Jasmine began passing out cigars and chocolates; both tied with blue ribbons. When she was asked what the occasion was, Jasmine proudly displayed a sparkling new engagement ring on her third finger, left hand, and announced: "It's a boy. 1.8 metres tall and ninety-five kilos." Honest to a fault!

Six

A New Broom Sweeps Clean.

Perseverance matters. You can't just keep changing partners and relationships as if the old ones don't matter. A new broom doesn't always sweep clean. Often, divorced people when they remarry or form back into another relationship think: "Thank goodness I've left all my problems behind. My previous X was really..." No! You will take some baggage into the next relationship. And that baggage is you.

I fully understand that divorce occurs. Some individuals should never have married to start with. It isn't true however that the more you try in marriage the better you get at it. Statistics can be contradictory, but let us briefly analyse them from two perspectives.

Firstly: Consider for a moment the 'generally quoted' average (even though I feel they are inflated), rounded off figures of the Western World[55] we all have often quoted, when it comes to marriage breakdown.

- *40%+ of first marriages end in divorce.*

- *60%+ of second marriages end in divorce.*

---

55 Statistics from five major Western countries gathered and constantly revised over time and cited in Marriage/Relationship Seminar of Ivan & Pauline Herald as one statistical measurement.

- **70%+ of third marriages end in divorce.**

- **In California around 94% of fourth marriages end in divorce**

Secondly: Shaunti Feldhahn, who is a Harvard-trained social researcher in her book *The Good News About Marriage*[56] strongly asserts that the general statics are wrong and often deliberately misleading. According to the USA Census Bureau 72% of those who have ever been married, are still married to their first spouse. As a highly trained statistical researcher Feldhahn puts the divorce rate of first marriages closer to 20-25%, through hard analytical investigation, rather than oft quoted 'gestimates.' For all marriages (including second marriages, and so on), Feldhahn asserts is in the 31-35%, not as popularised 60% and over.

Feldhahn's co-operative work with the Barna Group (who have in the past been seriously and deliberately misquoted as saying that the divorce rate was the same in the church as in the community), found that for people regularly attending church, their divorce rate dropped by 27%. Regular church attenders often referred to as 'Committed Christians' the divorce rate lowered overall by 25-50%.[57]

Whatever the absolutely accurate statistics divorce decimates, destroys and devastates. We have to persevere, to endure through the tough times as well as rejoicing together through the good. This is a commitment we make. I feel the outworking of this illustrates the deepening of intimacy between us. Our commitment to this principle will keep our love alive.

Referring to concepts dealt within the start of the book in the Section: *Introduction*, perseverance was noted as helping us keep the primary motivation going, and help us not slip back into awkward, self-defensive poor secondary behaviours.

Challenges can come at any time. In 1996 I was diagnosed with prostate cancer. The battle was on. Of the medical options back then the, side effects

56 Shaunti Feldhahn, The Good News About Marriage, Multnomah Books, 2014.

57 Ibid pp. 70-71. Also: https://catalystconference.com/read/everything-we-think-we-know-about-marriage-and-divorce-is wrong/?utm_source=catalyst+monthly&utm_medium=email&utm_content=title&utm_campaign=201405monthly

of radical surgery included a 70%+ chance of it seriously affecting sexual function. The primary alternative, radiotherapy, had then a 30%+ chance of having the same effect. Some urologists and oncology clinics in 1996 were revising that upward anything up to 50%.[58]

It was easy to become a little defensive about the whole issue. Pauline and I have always built our marriage on four levels of love based on four Greek terms (listed in no order of priority):

- **Agape** – Self-sacrificing love.

- **Phileo** – Affectionate, affirmative, companionship, responsive love.

- **Eros** – Physical, sexual, sensual love.

- **Storge** – Family *love,* the bond among mothers, fathers, sisters and brothers, and family bond of a couple etc.

Now, we faced the possibility of one of those areas possibly being wiped out, or seriously diminished. Understand that it was the perseverance, the commitment to deal positively with issues that come our way that carried us through. When I wanted to withdraw for various reasons to think things over Pauline refused to develop a secondary behaviour. Intimacy, deepening intimacy, caused us both to persevere through the battle.

We realised we had an incredibly strong Agape, Phileo, Eros and Storge love. Although the Eros was now under threat our relationship would survive even if the Eros partially or totally went down. One day we were sitting talking about this challenge (a great relationship can always talk sensibly about the battles we face together), and Pauline, referring to continuing sexual side of our relationship, in her usual understanding, loving way said: "Honey, it really doesn't matter."

---

58 These statistics have changed now in 2014 with radically improved methods of addressing prostate cancer. I only cite statistics as they 'were' in 1996.

Well that was just like red rag to a bull. I'm as red-bloodied as the next man. "Yes, it does," I maintained loudly. We both enjoyed the humour of the moment, but I knew what Pauline really meant. If anything went wrong then we still had a fabulous relationship, and the strength of who we are as a couple would carry us through.[59]

Some years ago Jeanette and Robert Lauer published the results from their powerful study[60]. They surveyed 351 couples that had been married fifteen years or more. Of the 351 couples, 300 said they were happily married. Each husband and wife responded individually to a questionnaire about marriage

The research was looking for indicators as to why their relationships had both lasted and proved to be happy. Out of thirty-nine important reasons, two of the four rated 'most important' for both the men and the women were: "Marriage is a long-term commitment," and "Marriage is sacred." And, no, it wasn't essentially a church-based survey. Note that both fall into the 'decision' area, rather than purely the 'desire' area. But, the application of these decisions was worked out in everyday demonstration of love.

Perseverance is absolutely essential. Lasting the distance and making changes to who we are, and how we respond, will make life with our partner so much the sweeter.

Slowly, and tragically, Hugh and Belinda have allowed their marriage to sink to new depths of criticism. Each blames the other. Neither accepts personal responsibility. At the insistence of their children, they go for counselling. Neither partner is prepared to persevere, bend, or yield.

Hugh promised to reign in his lavish expenditure, sit down with a financial counsellor with Belinda and develop a workable written budget. After a month, the idea of meeting with a financial counsellor and developing a budget has gone out of his mind and his attention. Belinda was not much better.

---

59 Footnote: Because you're all busting to know. No, nothing negative did happen in the Eros zone. But we had to face the possibility of sexual function loss, and face it together in love. But perseverance, coming out of our intimacy brought us through.

60 Til Death Do Us Part: How Couples Stay Together, Jeanette & Robert Lauer et al. Pub: Haworth Press, 1986.

Her assignment was to change the way and the tone in which she spoke to Hugh. No sooner are they in the car than Belinda is back to her old critically caustic ways of speaking and talking to Hugh.

Neither understands perseverance. Such isn't in their spirit to see this through. What are they demonstrating in this third area of marriage development? Stubbornness replaces openness. Bitterness grows in the darkness of the absence of genuine demonstrated love. 'Denial' of each other's needs in both of them replaces 'demonstration' as they collapse into inevitable marriage failure.

What Hugh and Belinda both demonstrate is a serious case of the 'Denial Disease.' They deny they have a problem. They deny each other's needs. They even deny their own needs to be fulfilled in a loving relationship with their spouse.

Can you guess the cost of this decision not to persevere? Have you thought through what a divorce will financially cost, physically cost, emotionally cost and socially cost?

If children are in the marriage what affect will marriage failure have on them? Isn't this a good reason to think through personal accountability, perseverance, and submission to a process of marital restoration?

Do you know what divorce costs us every year in Australia? The 2014 cost of divorce, for *every taxpayer* in Australia was $1,100[61]. This was stated as $14 billion a year in court costs, welfare, spouse, and child support. The figure has blown out $2 billion in the last two years alone. The Social Services Minister Kevin Andrews in May estimated: "each divorce was costing taxpayers at least $100,000."

This cost is supporting families in divorce crisis. The cost is only the measurable cost and obviously doesn't take into account the emotional cost or the ongoing effect on children and adults. Surely avoiding divorce is an economic benefit for the country, not just a social benefit.

Let us conclude this sub-section with an interesting illustration. A family of three children, now all married and with children of their own are trying to decide what present they will give to their parents for a significant wedding

---

61   Sunday Telegraph (Sydney), July 6th, pp. 9, sources statistics from The Attorney General's Department, The Department of Human Services and the Department of Social Services.

anniversary in a month's time. What could they buy parents who have retired early because they are so wealthy?

Because their parents have always been so caustic and bitter with each other in the way they talked to their spouse the family decided on the ultimate combined gift – a fully paid up course, extending over several sessions, with their city's most reputable, but expensive marriage guidance counsellor.

Initially, the parents appeared insulted, but their children won the day. But, it did take time.

"No Mum. No Dad. We want the best for you. You have all your life ahead, and you are now retired wealthy, though still young. You'll find this will help you to spend your time together in harmony, not fighting like we have seen continually. We only want to see you happy."

Their father commented caustically: "I supposed she could learn something." Typical! Now here they are in the counsellor's office. Furnishing and fixtures is very expensive. "I'm paying for all this," the husband thinks. Technically that wasn't true.

"Now, Elsie tell me about your relationship," the counsellor asks. Elsie begins, but no sooner gets her first point out, when her husband chips in with a rude cutting comment: "Women, you wouldn't have a brain in your head."

As much as the counsellor tries he cannot stop these rude continuing interjections by Jake, the husband. Often, the couple start fighting totally ignoring the counsellor sitting on the couch opposite.

Eventually, the counsellor turns to Jake, and tries to cut off the rude jibes, by asking him a question. Sure enough, Elsie starts straight back at her husband with her own rudeness as he answers.

"See, told you he was dead from the groin up." This went on for quite a while. Then in the midst of the couple having a huge fight, yelling at each other, the counsellor slams his hands on the arms of his couch, stands up very annoyed and comes across the floor and stands in front of both of them.

The couple are so involved in their personal argument that they haven't seen the counsellor move, or heard him, till he cups his hands putting them softly under Elsie's chin and slowly lifts her to a standing position. Then he, the counsellor, puts an impassioned kiss on her lips. He leaves her standing, softly swaying in the breeze, with just the wisp of a smile on her face.

Turning to Jake he says very annoyed: "I want you to make sure she gets that three times a week. Do you hear me, three times a week!" He marches across the room, still annoyed, to sit back now in his seat behind his desk. Jake looks back at Elsie who is still standing, smiling and still gently swaying.

"Ok," he says. "I'll bring her in on Mondays, Wednesdays, and Fridays if you like." I think he totally missed the point. No sense of perseverance.

Tragically Hugh and Belinda have crucified demonstrating genuine, tender love. Commitment to their marriage lies dead at the feet of their stubbornness. To fully revive this marriage they almost have to go right back to the first phase of 'Desire' and start all over again. However, tragically there seems little chance of that happening.

Seven

A Stitch In Time Saves Nine.

Why do we keep patching up old garments, when we can get something new? Understanding fully what the proverb is trying to say doesn't stop me looking at it from a different perspective. If something is coming to bits, sure it's good to repair it, but as in life why don't we think of something new.

I need to discover new things for Pauline, new ways to express love, things I haven't done before. Why can't we keep our relationship creatively, brilliantly fresh? I'm not sure I want to stitch up something that worked twenty, thirty years ago, but is now a little worn, even out-dated. I want something new.

We've been married over forty-eight years at the point of writing this book. Do you think to keep on doing what worked when we first married in 1966 is going to be all that helpful today? In some things yes. In other things no. Then what are the 'no' things? What can I change?

In 1966 or 1967 if we could get away for a weekend, camping or a caravan was about all we could afford, and what's more, a break like this was also quite normal then for many people, quite the done thing. You didn't tend to use motels/hotels as often as you do today.

Do you think I can get the Princess away camping today? Absolutely no way! Wild horses couldn't drag her there. Pauline maintains there are universal laws applicable to the Heralds and camping.

Firstly, Pauline insists, it always rains. Secondly, the toilets are definitely always at the opposite end to where we are allocated a camping site, and when needed it deliberately rains right as you start walking, and also there are no lights shining the way. And thirdly, they smell to high heavens, and you're never quite sure whether you're going to slip in and – I think you get the overall picture.

You have to understand something about my dear wife. Pauline has only very simple tastes – just the best! Pauline's idea of camping does involve 'counting the stars.' That is: the stars on the motel/hotel sign, not the sky.

Pauline loves the good quality, good standard motel/hotel. 'Five Star' all the way! Along the road of life I have constantly looked for ways to develop, give, and find something new for the relationship. In some way I'm not interested in keeping alive the old, when I can offer something better.

I must practise diligence in finding something new for the relationship. I must discover Pauline's uniqueness and aim to fulfil that need. Let me share another couple of personal illustrations.

The other day I bought Pauline a present. When she came home from helping run a community children's day-care program, as a volunteer, a coffee machine proudly sat on the kitchen bench. Pauline had wanted one for a while. On the card, I wrote: "This is a present for the special occasion of not having a special occasion to celebrate. It's a 'No Special Day Present.' Happy 'No Special Day.'" Finding new ways to say 'I love you' are fun.

One overseas speaking trip I was to be travelling alone. So, in wanting to send Pauline some flowers I arranged this through my now daughter-in-law. Bernice was then engaged to my son and was a florist.

"Listen Bernice, if I give you the money, the dates I want the flowers to arrive and the little message for the card, could you arrange for flowers to go to Pauline?"

"I would love to," Bernice said.

Great, I've got that sorted. When I was in America, in LA, I rang Pauline on a date the first lot of flowers were due. Just as she came onto the line I thought: "Oh, am I nineteen hours ahead in time or behind Sydney?" Flustered I didn't mention the flowers in case I was nineteen hours ahead and would spoil the surprise. When I got off the phone, I realised I was nineteen hours behind, and Pauline would already have had the flowers delivered yesterday. Yet, she had said nothing about the flowers. And, my wife really likes flowers.

So the next time I was on the phone I had to ask: "Honey, did you get any flowers the other day?"

"Oh, yes," was about her only response. The tone in her voice was one of complete complacency. Honest, I have had more enthusiasm out of a morgue slab. The very tone in her voice conveyed certain indifference.

When the second flowers were due I was then in the UK, I had to ask again if they had arrived. Again, there was that tone of indifference in her voice. Sure Pauline indicated she had got them, but there was absolutely no enthusiasm whatsoever, absolutely no description of the arrangement, which she normally gives. When I got home the third lot of flowers were still there on the dining room table.

"Oh, the flowers are nice," I said.

"Yes," Pauline said almost without intonation.

"Honey," I ventured, knowing I was going onto possible 'dangerous' territory. "Can I ask you something? What was wrong with the flowers? When I was in the USA and then the UK you didn't seem excited at all about either of the flowers I sent, and now your tone still doesn't reflect excitement for this lot."

Now, my dear wife, like most ladies, has a wondrous ability of not answering a question. Or, she rather answers a question with a question. Smart move!

"They were Bernice's flowers weren't they?"

"Yes," I offered, "I gave her the money, the dates and messages."

"No honey. They were Bernice's flowers," Pauline said again emphasising 'Bernice's.'

I still didn't get it, being as thick as two short bricks, so I attempted to explain again. "Yes, as I said, I gave Bernice the money, the dates and the messages."

"No honey, you're really not getting it. They were the flowers Bernice liked, not the flowers I like."

You see my Princess is a roses, carnations, iris, pretty spring flowers type of girl. Each of the arrangements that had been delivered was basically a dry flower arrangement. Pauline genuinely loved the brilliance Bernice had put into each design and presentation. Pauline thought that they were creatively magnificent and had told Bernice such. Innocently; however, I had just missed out on fulfilling Pauline's specific 'likes.'

You have to find what works for *you*.

Now, I know some lady out there might say: "I'd be happy with any flowers." However, that's another story, now isn't it? I had missed the mark for Pauline.

I find it a delight to find something new. Not stitch up old ideas, what worked yesterday, but finding the new. Keep the relationship alive with freshness, newness, and spontaneity.

Over the past two decades a group of family researchers in the United States have conducted many research projects in the area of family strengths. DeFrain et al.[62] and his colleagues have studied family strengths in twenty-seven countries.

They have discovered several viable models, of which we will only cite two. David Olson's Family Circumplex Model has three simple dimensions, existing in a healthy marriage.

These are:

- *Cohesion.*

- *Flexibility.*

- *Communication.*

62 Marriage And Families: Intimacy, Diversity, and Strengths, John DeFrain, David Olson, Linda Skogrand, Pub: Mayfield, Mountain View, California, 2000.

The Stinnett and DeFrain view called Family Strengths Model consisted of six extended qualities being:

- ***Commitment to the family.***

- ***Appreciation and affection for each other***

- ***Positive communication patterns***

- ***Enjoyable time together***

- ***A sense of spiritual wellbeing.***

- ***Connection.***

Notice the importance of relationship values instead of the older view of roles. We need to be smart enough to find what works and duplicate it.

Amar's shops were both going very well. Both he and Mia talked of opening another two in other cities. Amar's resolve to spend quality time with Mia had not diminished.

Saturday and Sunday had become their special time. Because of their cultural heritage little signs of affection were not generally displayed in public. However, both Amar and Mia were determined to set up their own culture, a culture of a happy and lasting marriage.

Amar would deliberately hold Mia's hand in public; a display of love between men and women rarely endorsed from their particular part of India where they had come from.

Once a relative attempted to correct them. Amar was quick to correct the individual and the criticism. Mia beamed with pride at her man defying the norm to produce the best in their marriage. Though they enjoyed their Indian heritage, they never let their background dictate the joy or progress of their own relationship.

Clearly Amar believed in demonstrating his love on a regular basis. Generally, such displays are more productive when they have a none-expectant return implication. Amar wasn't demonstrating love to 'get.' He was giving love to verify his loving heart.

Both Amar and Mia worked hard on finding what really worked in each other. Mia loved being away in the setting of nature's beauty, so at least once every four or five weeks Amar would find somewhere unique, tranquil, exotic and restful.

Mia particularly loved Falls Lodge, and many a relaxing weekend was spent near the magnificent waterfalls. In winter it was lattes and slow lunches, with a small log fire burning behind them, on the lodge wooden patios and various terraces, facing the three waterfalls. Reading and chatting in the winter sunshine were special.

In summer there was swimming in the beautiful cool waters, avoiding the intensity of the summer sun. Falls Lodge had many shady covered patios adjacent to the waterfalls. They each had deck chairs that opened out for full relaxation in the luxuriant shade. Brilliant coloured birds made their presence felt in idle chatter and cheekily trying to grab crumbs.

Amar loved just reading, walking, and relaxing – anywhere would suit him, though like Mia he did particularly like Falls Lodge. There were magnificent forest walks around the lodge. Relaxing with Mia was a particular delight. Mia would indulge that need. In relaxing with Amar in their room, she made the Kama Sutra look primitive.

Mia also loved massages. Amar specially did a course in massage just so he could fulfil that need. His massages were not sexually orientated, but Mia-orientated, giving her the pleasure she found in them, without any subtle demands.

Flowing from both of them was a passionate desire to meet the other's needs, to demonstrate their love, in whatever way they could. They were more than diligent; they made giving a lifestyle, requiring nothing back. It demonstrated their deepening intimacy, because it became a natural response as well as desire.

Giving warmed Mia and Amar emotionally. Satisfying emotional well being filled their marriage as they concentrated on satisfying each other. They found what worked. And, they worked at what they found.

Eight

GARBAGE IN, GARBAGE OUT.

Contessa phoned Graham at work from home: "Hi honey, how's your day?" They chatted for a while. "Look I'm coming into town. As you know, I've got that appointment on the Lord Mayor's committee for our town's Christmas celebrations. How about lunch? Have you got time?"

"Sure. How about 1.00pm at The Tea Rooms?"

"Ok, honey, meet you there. But, I've got to be away by 1.45pm for my 2.00pm appointment. See ya..." Both felt happy to catch up for lunch.

All didn't go to plan. Graham got caught up in an intense emergency strategy session at work, called at 12.30pm, and clean forgot about his lunch appointment till the meeting concluded at 2.00pm. All the time, as required, his phone was switched off. Contessa had left The Tea Room at 1.45pm and left a message on Graham's phone just before 2.00pm as she walked into her Lord Mayor's committee meeting. Contessa then switched her phone off.

It wasn't their best of days. Graham realised he had blown it. Picking up some roses on the way home he stuck his hand in the front door and waggled the roses as he pushed the front doorbell several times. Contessa came down the hall and realised the implications.

There on the front porch Graham was playfully on his knees begging for forgiveness, kissing her feet, fooling around. Contessa could do nothing but laugh. On his feet again he held her round the waist and as they walked inside he apologised again.

"I'm really, really sorry honey. There is no excuse for forgetting and leaving you sitting there. I got caught up in an intense strategy meeting that was called at the last minute, and that was it. I know I should have phoned, but it was a pressured meeting and it clean went out of my head, as I had to present some points of view. I understand however, that's no excuse for my beautiful Spanish mistress," he said as he playfully kissed her neck.

"You're forgiven. Didn't get lunch though, only a coffee. In fact, I haven't eaten since. You owe me! And owe me big time," Contessa said laughing as she reached for a vase for the roses.

"Done!" Graham said. "We have a 7.30pm booking at The Fallen Stag for dinner tonight. I've booked a window seat, candlelight, the works."

Contessa squealed with joy as she went off to get ready. She had skilfully arranged the brilliant yellow roses and took them with her to the bedroom.

We all make mistakes. Why is saying 'sorry' so hard for some? They discovered in the 1950s that: "I'm sorry" were the two hardest words in the English language to say. For some people I don't think much has changed over sixty to seventy years later.

Don't let garbage in and you won't get garbage out. Graham and Contessa have made a commitment not to hold grudges, to share their hurts and how they felt, and to always say they're sorry.

Now, those commitments have become personal fulfilments in their life. They practised and demonstrated each area. Keeping accounts short helps them not to brood on past garbage that is not cleared out.

Now let's consider if they had not positively dealt with the irritating issue. Instead of producing a pearl within them, they could let the annoyance ulcerate their relationship. Contessa could take a greater offence than intended. Graham could get upset with her, and before you know you have World War III over what – a forgotten lunch appointment.

Deepening intimacy releases emotional security and operates from the strength of our emotional being. Saying sorry is natural not defensive to Graham and Contessa. Things happen. Why take incidents to a level never intended.

For every action, there is an equal and corresponding reaction. Sow to emotional security and reap deepening intimacy.

I am sure we all want the best for our children. Then, we need to take personal responsibility for the relationship to ensure our commitment to each other not only works, but also works well. Glenn Stanton, social research analyst and author of *Why Marriage Matters*[63], shares solid reasons to believe in marriage after having examined one hundred and thirty empirical studies associated with Professor H. Coombs, Professor of Behavioural Sciences at the University of California, Los Angeles.

Briefly it was discovered that children born out of wedlock or affected by separation and divorce are more likely to experience:

- *Lower new-born health;*

- *Slower cognitive and verbal development;*

- *Lower educational standards;*

- *Lower levels of job attainment;*

- *More behavioural and emotional problems;*

- *Increased dependency on welfare;*

- *Lower financial wellbeing;*

- *Increased exposure to crime;*

---

63 Why Marriage Matters, Glenn Stanton. Pub: NAV Press, 1997.

- *At greater risk of sexual abuse.*

- *Marital problems of their own.*

So in short we may make mistakes, but let's not pass them on. We surely want the best future for our children. So, don't make lame excuses for your mistakes. Deal with them.

Don't be like the motorist making excuses for his driving, who was stopped by a police radar unit. After being asked why he was exceeding the sixty-kilometre speed limit he said: "I was temporarily overcome by a wave of nostalgia. I thought the speed limit was eighty."

Conclusion To: Demonstration, The Real Test Of A Relationship.

Passionate desire is essential, but desire alone cannot sustain. Add to desire a total resolve, and decision-making commitment to the relationship, come what may, and the relationship starts to mature. So now the 'decision side' of the relationship has reinforced the 'desire side.'

In this Section of the book we have been dealing with the 'demonstration side' or dimension of the relationship. Deepening intimacy further develops the maturing relationship. Natural emotional responses are triggered to keep the relationship buoyant, alive, and fulfilling.

This demonstration starts to become more relaxed and more natural. We shouldn't need to be forcibly proving our love. Love should flow out of us naturally. For that to occur we must deal with whom we are. When our esteem is strong we want to fulfil another, to help them reach their fullness. We want to give of ourself.

This determination must drive us to make the right choices and feed the relationship with pro-life values. Genuine commitment refuses to let 'denial' replace demonstration. Constant demonstration overcomes a 'denial' mentality. In demonstration we choose to live emotionally whole, cognitively sound, socially balanced and in every other way mature adults.

This level of living is life injecting. Truly the Beauty, not the Beast is beginning to glow. People can see the transformation of a couple into that essential essence of a truly loving marriage.

Section 4

DETERMINATION, CHOICES AND DESTINY.

Life is all about choices. Sadly we don't always make the right ones. Sometimes the choices we make are deliberate, at other times we slip, glide, and often by default fall into so many decisions. Occasionally, because we didn't make a decision, this became our decision. We are stuck with indecision as a decision. Consider they are our choices nevertheless. And, we must 'own' them.

We must also realise that there are always consequences associated with every decision we make or don't make. What does the ancient text of the then wandering Hebrew nation say: "I have put before you this day life and good, death and evil…therefore choose life that both you and your descendants might live."[64]

I want my children, grandchildren, and those beyond me to know Ivan and Pauline chose 'good' and 'life' for their marriage and family, and that we were always deeply in love. Therefore, I must deliberately choose 'life.' I must deliberately choose 'good' as a conscious act of my will, and in so doing pass it on, like an indescribable heritage, to those who come after us.

The greatest inheritance I can give my children and grandchildren is to love their mother and grandmother! Now, I know they may be hoping for another type of inheritance, but that's another issue. A stable and loving

---

64 Deuteronomy 30 verse 19.

marriage and family are the most valued of gifts. And that gift needs to be visibly observed.

My choices mould my destiny. I am determined to offer the best. These are conscious choices I must make now.

So, in a conscious reflection of the first three dimensions I determine, or choose to keep desire and passion in my relationship. I choose to make proactive decisions about the issues that come up to potentially destroy our relationship. Finally, I choose to daily demonstrate intimacy in my relationship.

These are my choices. This is my determination. My decisions determine the destiny of my marriage and my family. Deeply rooted within these choices and determination is my capacity and willingness to change. Remember change does not come readily or comfortably to any of us.

Change begins with a decision. Continual change, or its absence, is the reason why you are what you are, or your relationship is what it is. Have you decided and are you committed to doing something about it?

Continuing change is not an event. Such is a process. Events are the catalyst. Change is the agent. You must be committed to the process of change and understand its time constraints.

Though it might sound contradictory and an oxymoron the only constant in the journey of life is change. Change is the essence of the maturation of not only yourself, but also your relationship.

Incredible adaptability is necessary in the journey of your relationship. When you have a clear vision of where you want your relationship to go, you begin to realise that the discipline necessary to get you there is often a healthy bye-product of that vision.

A stubborn person will always be an ignorant person. You won't change until you're willing to be confronted by the truth and convinced such is the truth. You will also not change till you're confronted by yourself and make positive choices to change. All truth is confrontational.

It takes courage to change. Once you make that commitment decisions translate to energy. Remember that when change is necessary, not to change is destructive. 'Changes' twin sister; 'determination' must follow your decision.

Determination is outworked through discipline. Discipline is part of the re-sources of life that will bring us through tough times.

The opposite of determination is 'defensiveness.' How tragic when cou-ples breed 'defensiveness,' instead of a healthy 'determination' in their mar-riage. Clearly in the lives of the few couples in this book, whose marriages are not working, you can see their 'defensiveness.' How disastrous for them and as a role model for their families.

Throughout history, good and bad leaders have evidenced determination. In many cases, dogged determination was what brought them through to suc-cess and/or notoriety.

The mighty Carthaginian general Hannibal was one of the few military leaders to lead his troops and defeat the Romans in many significant battles. He took the battle to the Romans, right into Italy.

Hannibal defied his generals who said that they couldn't cross the Alps, especially with elephants and cavalry. In a statement that has outlived him Hannibal said: "We will either find a way or make one."[65]

Consequently in 218BC, Hannibal led the 20,000 infantry, 6,000 cavalry, and 40 elephants across the Alps in just 15 days, when they said it couldn't be done.

In marriage we need that same determination – *we will either find a way, or make one!*

So this final Section is about 'determination.' How determined are you to:

- *Firstly: Enthuse your relationship with passion and desire.*

- *Secondly: Make firm conscious positive decisions to confront what comes against your marriage.*

- *Thirdly: Demonstrate daily the growing love that you have for each other?*

- *How determined are you really?*

---

65 Julian Thompson. Call To Arms. Pub: Quercus Books, London, 2009. Pg. 18.

- *What price will you be prepared to pay?*

- *What will you put on the line for your relationship?*

  Remember the price of a failed marriage is much higher than you ever imagined.

Let us explore this dynamic of determination as it affects the three important Sections we have already dealt with and see its interaction in the lives of the seven couples, whose stories are threaded throughout this work.

One

GETTING TO THE CORE OF ISAAC'S APPLE.

The year was 1705. Christmas day was only a few weeks away. Another birthday for Isaac. The world had already acclaimed the fame and importance of Sir Isaac Newton. His book *Philosophiae Naturalis Principia Mathematica* (Mathematical Principles of Natural Philosophy) had been first published in 1687.

Isaac Newton's knighthood by Queen Anne in her visit to Trinity College, Cambridge in April of 1705 had catapulted the reputation and standing of this humble lad from Woolsthorpe.

Isaac had moved from Cambridge in 1696 to take up a post of Warden Of The Mint. In 1703 Isaac Newton had become President of the Royal Society and was re-elected annually till his death. With his knighthood, he was now famous. However, Isaac loved his occasional trips back to Cambridge.

Guest lectures had brought him here again.

Isaac was now almost 63 years of age. In a break from lectures, one Sunday afternoon, Isaac strolled to the resting place of his favourite apple tree. The tree looked much older. "Don't we all," Isaac thought. A light snow covering on the hilltop, though thick on the fields, sat upon the ground from a mid November snowfall. Isaac looked at the apple tree.

"Hello, old friend." The tree was now aged, like Isaac felt. He patted the apple tree like patting the shoulder of a lifelong acquaintance. A smile spread across his face.

"The world thinks I'm famous because of my Three Laws of Motion. However, they just don't realise that I was also talking about relationship as well. Oh, well, it's just the flip side of the same coin," Isaac thought as he recalled the investiture of his knighthood some months earlier in April.

Certainly, his laws were all about motion. Because of his profound interest in gravity since the mid to late 1660's, the ideas had been easier to express and hide relationship issues in mathematical and motion terms.

"But Oh, how they apply to people," he muttered aloud.

Isaac pulled his coat around his neck to ward off a chilling snow-soaked breeze that was gently blowing over the brow of the hill. The trees were leafless. Occasional icicles hung like early Christmas decorations. The sun shimmered through them, giving off sparkling glints of a brilliant spectrum of rainbow colours, as they slowly dripped.

Isaac was just about to turn and walk back to his lodgings when, to his pleasure, he spotted his favourite couple crossing the paddock where the bull once lived. 'Bartholomew The Bull' had long since gone and now thick snow covered the fallow ground.

Andrew and Joan had remained good friends with Isaac Newton. Their family and love for each other had grown. Now, a family of five children playfully threw snowballs at each other, with the occasional one especially and accurately aimed at their father.

Isaac watched as Andrew playfully chased the eldest son now twenty years old and a blacksmith by trade. Both were throwing snowballs at each other as fast as they could make them. The other children joined in on their brother's side as Joan retreated to the safety of sitting on the stile with their youngest daughter and their oldest son's fiancé.

Eventually, Andrew had seen and recognised the lone figure up near the apple tree and he waved as they all made their way towards Isaac. The children reached 'Uncle Isaac' first, as he had affectionately become known.

"Well now," said Andrew as he shook hands, "It's no longer Professor, but 'Sir Isaac' that I gotta call you now. We were at your investiture of your knighthood at Trinity you know, but couldn't get near you, to congratulate you, because of the crowd of important people with her majesty the queen there. Of course we didn't get an invite to the food hall. Her majesty's guards kept us away from you.

Great to see you again my friend."

Both men laughed as they recalled the past and together, with the family, they walked back to the village just before Cambridge where Andrew and Joan now lived. Then Isaac would continue to his lodgings at the university.

Isaac Newton had often thought about Andrew, Joan, and their growing brood. What a beautiful and perfect example of growing love in a relationship. Now their eldest son, Joseph, soon to be married with the reading of the banns already commenced, was engaged to and keeping company with one of the girls from the village. Isaac could see Joseph duplicating the same tender care of his fiancé, Sarah that he had seen in his father well over twenty years ago. Like was breeding like.

His academic friends often disappointed Isaac. John was now dead, and Mary was frail. Isaac understood that even though they stayed together till his death their marriage had died long ago. It is just that they didn't have an official funeral for the marriage. The marriage had been dead, stinking, behind their insufferable veneer of public acceptance.

Edward and Elizabeth had divorced, an unbelievable disgrace for the early 1700's. Each had bitterly accused the other. Isaac didn't want to be involved with such bitterness or in continuing disappointing relationships.

Late that night Isaac sat in his room at the university reflecting over his three laws of relationship. "I must extend them one day," he mused as he picked up his quill and wrote in his journal further thoughts about people, marriage, relationship, and choices.

"Now what was it Andrew was saying this afternoon? Oh, that's right. 'Professor, ya know love is like energy. We can't make love or destroy it. The best we can do is to transfer that emotional energy one to another. But, we need to make sure its positive emotional energy. We need to, ya know, give it away.

Love multiplies naturally Isaac, in acts of love received. Then, as it multiplies more can be given away. I've seen some of your friends Professor. They tried to create love for themselves in things, instead of transferring what love they naturally had. I don't trys to create love for myself Professor, I trys to give it away.' What a wise friend you are Andrew," Isaac thought.

Grabbing his writing quill Isaac scribbled: Love (energy) can be transformed in various ways, but cannot be created or destroyed.

"I think that might catch on in the future," Isaac mused.

Isaac's last entry for the night was just as insightful from the words of Joan. One day, whilst sharing a meal with them in their humble cottage, Joan had captured a key truth.

"Professor, we's won't let our marriage run down. We's keep it alive. The trouble with many is they don't feed their marriage; they don't replenish their love."

She moved over to the fireplace to fetch meat for their meal keeping warm.

"Look here governor at me fire. The only way I's can cook yous this meal is to keep the fire burning. My fire left to itself will go out. It will run out Professor. I got to feed the fire with more fuel. Same with marriage." Again, there were pearls of wisdom from a humble woman, who seemed to understand so much more than many of Isaac's educated friends.

Isaac's pure white swan's-wing feather quill scrawled a final note: Any system (relationship or marriage) left to itself will decay, like the fire going out. "Um, entropy. That's the name. I'm sure that will catch on someday," said Isaac staring at the flickering candle.

Now the President of the Royal Society and Warden Of The Mint tucked himself into bed. Fame had not dulled his sense of humour, or his appreciation of good honest and genuine people.

"One day those ideas will be important. Someone will develop them I'm sure," Isaac thought again as he drifted off to sleep.

In the very late 1790s and through to the early 1820s those ideas did formalise. Nevertheless, do they refer only to physics, chemistry, mathematics, or only the sciences, or are they not equally important to relationship?

Later The Laws Of Thermodynamics[66] as they would eventually become known would revolutionise science. Hadn't Andrew and Joan understood some of their more expansive principles in practical relationship-building truths? In basics one of the Laws Of Thermodynamics, and its application to marriage states:

> *"Energy* (or love in relationship) *can be transformed in various ways, but cannot be created or destroyed. Any system* (relationship/marriage) *left to itself will decay [Entropy]."*

Successful relationships incorporate choices, wise, smart, and life-injecting choices. Happy couples have a steel-like determination that refuses any standard but the best for their relationship.

> *The Challenge: The fire in any marriage can go out. It should be our resolute determination to make the right healthy choice to keep it alive, hot, and a maturing shining example to those who come after us.*

---

66 The Laws Of Thermodynamics: We clearly understand Isaac Newton didn't develop the one we have referred to. Count Rumford (born Benjamin Thompson) showed, about 1797, that mechanical action could generate indefinitely large amounts of heat, so challenging the caloric theory. The first established thermodynamic principle, which eventually became The Second Law Of Thermodynamics, was formulated by Sadi Carnot, during 1824. By 1860, as formalized in the works of those such as Rudolf Clausius and William Thomson, two established principles of thermodynamics had evolved, the first principle and the second principle, later restated as thermodynamic laws. However, wider reading and research on the Laws Of Thermodynamics accredits the foundational principles and understanding to the continuation of the work of several previous mathematicians and physicists, inclusive of Isaac Newton.

Two

BETTER THE DEVIL YOU KNOW,
THAN THE ONE YOU DON'T.

What a load of rubbish. Firstly, to refer to our spouse as the 'devil we know' illustrates that few if any positive changes are going on. Such an attitude is definitely not seeing or producing the Beauty in our spouse, but assuredly the Beast.

Many individuals struggle to change their spouse, not themself. This reminds me of a man that drove past a line of over fifty men standing single file behind two hearses. Just behind the last hearse was a black limousine with the hood up, obviously with engine trouble. The man pulled to the side of the road, got out and offered to help. However, they were just satisfactorily finishing repairs. A huge dog was hanging out the widow of the limousine, appearing to supervise the repairs.

The man inside the limousine thanked the man, but just before he walked off the helpful driver said. "Pardon me sir. But, I have never before seen such a long line of men behind a hearse. Was the deceased an important person?"

"Well, in the first hearse up there is my Mother-in-law. The dog sitting next to me here killed her."

"Oh, I'm terribly sorry," said the man. "But, what about the second hearse?"

"In the second hearse is my interfering neighbour, my Mother-in-law's sister who always took my Mother-in-law's side and reported to her constantly anything she thought I did wrong, even when I wasn't doing anything. Then my Mother-in-law would abuse me. And, my dog next to me here killed her also."

"I'm so sorry," said the man as he turned to walk back to his car. After three steps, he stopped and turned around. "Excuse me sir, but would it be possible to borrow your dog for a while?"

The man in the limousine looked back casually and replied: "Get in line."

Somehow I don't think that illustrates trying to really change bad situations. Consider however, that this does illustrate how many people think today.

The proverb in the heading above smacks of just putting up with the bad relationship you've got. Making no effort to change pervades the expression.

Change isn't always comfortable, nor does it come naturally to any of us. Not that Hugh and Belinda knew that. Lack of patience with each other bordered on childishness. Now grandparents, they evidenced more patience with the little wilful, sometimes naughty, yet cute ways of their grandchildren than with each other.

One day when picking up their children, after Hugh and Belinda had been minding them, one of their daughters had left exasperated after hearing their parents in another row.

"Honestly Mum, Dad. When will you grow up? Arguing is all we heard when we were kids. And, I surely don't want my children exposed to it. I want them to respect their grandparents. Do you know what Jessica asked me the other day? 'Why do Grandma and Grandad fight all the time?' You really are impossible. If you can't stop arguing in front of the children, I'll have to find somewhere else to mind them." She stormed out of the house furious, children in tow. She slammed the front door. I wonder where she learned that?

Hugh and Belinda's relationship had sunk to new depths of indifference. Though it seems hard to believe, they were now almost set in concrete in their insecurities. They were now determined to win each argument, each battle, and each encounter.

The ingrained first response of both Hugh and Belinda was now 'defensiveness.' Positive 'determination' to build their life together has been given the flick. This destructive 'defensiveness' had years ago replaced their original primary response of determination. Defensiveness was sadly now Hugh and Belinda's first response.

Understand that positive 'determination' is the key issue of this last Section, but not destructive determination. Never have Hugh or Belinda lasted the thirty to sixty days necessary to change their bad habits. Sure, for peace sake, they tried a few times. However, their motivation was wrong. We should want to change for the good of our spouse, the relationship, and ourself, not just for peace sake.

Saturday morning found them furiously arguing again.

"Well, it is not my damn fault the jaguar was repossessed," Belinda screamed. "If you could only handle money better we wouldn't be in this mess. You never think it's your problem. You always blame me."

Belinda was livid with rage. Her whole body language, facial expressions and tone of voice were as hostile as you could get.

Hugh had heard enough. "Yea, and you just blame me. Have you seen these credit card statements? You're always out spending. Everyone knows you've got a serious problem with spending." Hugh made his point slapping two of Belinda's fancy shopping bags, still sitting on the dining room table, filled with more expensive clothes. He paced around angrily.

"You're just like your mother. She was just as bad. Everybody knows she had money problems. Don't know why I bothered marrying you." Hugh made his last insulting point with venom as he went and sat in the lounge recliner, instantly picking up the paper and stuck his head firmly into the sports page. This was his cop-out. Hugh's modern day cave.

That was the last straw for Belinda. She stormed out the room. You guessed right she slammed the door on her exit. Screeching gravel was heard as Belinda filled with fury backed out the pebble based driveway in a consuming rage, rocketing backwards out, off to see the kids, to shop, anywhere but here.

The screech of tires, the sickening crash, the sound of glass, metal, and life breaking up deafened the air. Hugh went white as he realised what had happened. Racing out the house he saw Belinda's car effectively impaled front and back from cars from both sides of the road both hitting her car simultaneously at just over 60kmph each. Belinda's car was partly torn in two. Death took centre stage as Belinda and one other driver died. Destructive anger had taken other unsuspecting lives.

What had an arrogant, hard-nosed determination to win cost Hugh and Belinda?

We started in Section 1 looking at the need to keep desire or passion, fun, and romance alive.

Within Section 2 we reinforced that by bolstering up the relationship with specific decision-making processes, developing an unshakable commitment to build a great relationship, especially when difficult times came.

Section 3 found us exploring a deepening intimacy by couples demonstrating self-sacrificing love frequently in the relationship.

Finally, here in Section 4, we are addressing determination.

Hugh and Belinda let their relationship tragically sink to an inflexible position of daily 'Win-Lose' battles. What we should determine to produce is a 'Win-Win,' not Win-Lose,' relationship. We should be sold out on producing nothing but the best in our spouse and for our spouse.

We are not hapless victims of life. Choices are made with our life and for our life, and we must either suffer the consequences of bad choices or reap the rich rewards of positive ones.

Psychologists at the University in Seattle[67], Washington, USA observed, over an extended period of time, how one hundred and twenty-four couples that had been married nine months or less approached and interacted in a disagreement. Their research was so thorough that the researchers believed that they could then predict within three minutes of a couple interacting the propensity of that couple towards divorce.

The couples who started arguments with negative words, gestures, body and facial expressions are more likely to divorce after six years the research had shown.

---

67   Research of Washington University and Gottman Institute reported in Family Process magazine (USA) and The Townsville Bulletin Oct. 6th, 1999, pg. 21.

How do you interact when tension is in the air? Do you and your gestures become hostile? Or, are you able to in a calm and committed way work through to resolve differences?

There is what I call the 'Principle Of Exclusion' in conflict management and it is easily applicable to couples. We must, if we want our marriage to survive, be smart enough to 'exclude' certain things out of our conflict management methods as a couple. 'Like what?' you might ask. Let me suggest what we should exclude.

Firstly: When conflict is in the air certain words must be excluded, such as 'Always,' 'Everyone' and 'Never.' These are inflammatory. As words they can only be defined by themself. They are exaggerates. They don't give any room for an alternate view as they're absolutes.

Notice in Hugh and Belinda's dialogue above how they use them with destructive results.

Secondly: Eliminate certain phrases. "You're just like your mother," and other like inflammatory phrases don't help. Exclude them. That's why we call it the Principle Of Exclusion. Did you see this area used by Hugh?

Thirdly: Exclude certain actions. Slamming doors (Belinda's favourite action), checking out behind a newspaper (Hugh's withdrawal and childish ignoring technique), getting out the house and driving off in rage (Belinda's last tragic action), and other equally destructive actions all need to be excluded.

You have to honestly look at 'what' you're doing. Then, after recognising some areas as negative and destructive to the relationship then seek to exclude them. Banish them from your way of dealing with your emotions, your spouse and yourself.

Finally: Destructive emotions need to be eliminated (anger or complete withdrawal as just two of many examples).

Sadly, Hugh and Belinda wont get another chance to repair their relationship. But, **you** have an opportunity now to make the right choices, to evidence your determination to turn any hostile energy into positive energy.

You have latent energy within you. Don't say I can't love again. Rubbish! Transfer the energy you have now, which may be negative, into positive actions. Determine if necessary to go back to Section 1 and start creating desire and passion again.

You can do it.

Three

EVERY CLOUD HAS A SILVER LINING.

No! Good doesn't 'always' come out of every bad situation. Good isn't an accident of occurrence, but a result of choice. There has to be a firm resolute heart to turn our scars into stars. We have to make choices, carefully thought out choices, and then evidence a strong determination to fulfil them, but not at each other's expense like the illustration below.

A woman and her husband had to interrupt their holiday and visit the dentist urgently. "I want a tooth pulled, and I don't want Novocain because I'm in a big hurry. I've got another flight in two hours," the woman demanded. "Just extract the tooth as quickly as possibly so we can be on our way to the airport."

The dentist was impressed. "You're certainly a courageous woman," he said. "Which tooth is it?" The woman turned to her husband and said: "Show him your tooth, dear."

Working through the tough times equates to resilience. Walsh[68] in one study defines resilience as: "the ability to withstand and rebound from crisis and adversity." The study showed strong marriages, and families were found

---

68 Walsh's 1998 work cited in: Searching For Family Resilience, Simone Silberberg. Family Matters, No. 58, Autumn, 2001, Australian Institute Of Family Studies.

to be able to adapt to changing circumstances and have a positive attitude towards the challenges of family life.

Such families deal with the challenges of life by means of communication, talking things through with each other, supporting each other in times of need and/or seeking outside support when solutions are beyond the family's capability to deal with the situation; and togetherness – pulling together to form a united front and to find solutions.

Above all the study showed that the couples did not isolate, withdraw, and attempt to solve their problem alone. Overcoming difficulties requires joint action.

John and Julie have called their marriage quits. Finally, Julie became aware of John's affair with Sandra, not that Julie cared much. His adultery really became an excuse to end a painful marriage, with a seeming justifiable reason. Her friends at her various social clubs and her relatives all commiserated with her.

"That *#^*! John," was the common utterance for such a cad. Clearly, it was just an excuse. Julie was just as responsible for the death of their love, now their marriage, not that such ever excuses adultery.

Julie ranted and raved. Tears flowed. How strange that she became so emotional about the death of a relationship in which Julie was so lacking in emotion. Sadly she evidenced more emotion in the finalisation of their marriage than often ever in it. As is common with many wounded women Belinda was more concerned about what John had promised the new love in his life.

In Arthur Millers stunning play 'The Crucible,' Elizabeth Proctor, wife of the play's hero, John Proctor, makes a significant poignant statement about the power of sexual betrayal. Having just learnt of the affair, which John had with a servant girl, John's wife challenged him about the promise, which he had made the girl.

"What promise?" demands John. Her answer is profound, and both scary and illuminating.

"In every bed, there is a promise made."

Any system/marriage left to itself will decay. Life and momentum have to actively be kept alive in the relationship. Neither John nor Julie had injected life into the relationship in years. Not that they would tell anybody, but separate bedrooms had been their choice for over four years.

They didn't attempt to overcome difficulties, trials, and the common detractors together in their marriage. When Julie was diagnosed with a lump in her breast John seemed indifferent.

Though John never said it, but 'You'll get over it,' was his callous implied attitude, if not in words. He didn't even go with her to the hospital when Julie had the biopsy taken, or to the doctors who gave her the report that the lump was benign.

Julie struggled through alone. This is something no one should ever have to do without support. That indifference in John birthed a loathsome resentment in Julie. When she most needed her man, despite all their differences, where was he?

In a time, when John could have shown his 'determination' to love, care, and be there for Julie, the best he could produce was 'defensiveness.' Isn't it sad that intelligent people can be so dumb?

It seemed like they were on an inevitable collision course with divorce. Sadly, they didn't care.

Had there ever been glimmers of hope? Yes. Once, on a holiday away in the Caribbean John and Julie did things together. Fun, started to creep back into their daily program. Gentleness towards each other started to surface. They sat for hours at restaurants, amidst the coastal beauty of the islands, the sand, the palms and the clear aquamarine sea sparkling in the setting sun. They enjoyed moonlight candlelight dinners and suppers, chatting about everything.

John brought Julie breakfast in bed and the paper to read most mornings. Once a red fragrant rose was on her breakfast tray. Twice together they went sailing having so much fun. They enjoyed a Caribbean feast around an outdoor fire, cooked in the old Caribbean indigenous tribal ways in the ground, in one of the old villages. Getting home late, they were exhilarated, happy and excitedly talked together for another hour before retiring. Sexual frequency increased as they genuinely sought to fulfil their spouse.

Sadly, the holiday was too short. That small ray of light, just peeping through the opening opportunity, was quickly extinguished as they returned home to their boring routines.

They slammed the window of hope shut as they carelessly lapsed back into recriminatory behaviour. If only they had pushed through, offered genuine apologies, kept fun alive and invited tenderness and forgiveness to join in as friends. Tragically, they were personally fixated on, and determined to 'win.' Win for themselves, not for each other. So 'Win-Lose' came knocking at the door and 'Win-Win' was thrown out on its ear.

Charles Cooley (1864-1929), a noted American sociologist, developed what is called: 'The Looking Glass Self.' In brief, Cooley states:

"That we will think, and therefore act, according to what we think that the most important person in the world to us, thinks about us."

It is an illuminating and insightful concept.

John and Julie stopped being the most important people in the world to each other. When they did give a thought to what each other thought, it generally was not pleasant. So, what did they think and therefore act out? Their lives reflected the unpleasantness they were sure was being thought by their spouse about them.

Certainly, early in his affair John had found passion and desire with Sandra. Predictably that waned. Sandra moved on. There were more important executives to pursue. Another step up the ladder.

As is often the case for the Sandra's of life, her actions were always about professional vocational advantage. Her goal - one day she would be CEO. The affair with John essentially was all about where John could take her.

John's social life drifted nebulously, fulfilled in little except managing his portfolio of properties. Boredom set in.

The divorce was bitter. Property division was painful. The lawyers did very well out of the whole mess. Strange isn't it that John spent more in legal fees and taxes on property subdivision with Julie than he every invested in Julie as surprise holidays or thoughtful gifts.

Another couple's lifelong dream bites the dust because they had no determination in the relationship. Their lack of determination became their determination.

Four

WHERE'S THERE'S A WILL, THERE'S A WAY.

Actually, someone smart once said: "Where there's a will, there are the relatives."

Is it just 'one way' we are looking for, or many ways? There are hundreds of ways we can give, share, create, and make love. There has to be many ways to look at any situation.

When Pauline and I need to address something, there is my way, her way, and then the right way. That can often be an integration of the best of both of our ways, and a purposeful leaving aside of the weakness of both of our ways.

Christians often use the term 'one flesh' when describing oneness together in a good marriage. Though some ill-informed Christians will claim this concept relates to bearing children; 'one flesh' is really dealing with the whole intimacy of the relationship in every area. Together we can demonstrate a stronger entity together than just including the individual addition of the two sides of the relationship.

In the corporate realm, they often call this 'synergy.' Whatever the term you prefer, we should be aiming to produce a stronger 'us' than we are alone. Together we should be, and can be an indomitable force.

If I represent 'X' units of potential for a great marriage and Pauline also represents an 'X' potential, then you would think together we would be '2X.' In actual fact together we can be '20X', '25X', or more. Together, merged into oneness, we are infinitely more potent than we could be in isolation or even just added together.

Originally, Euclid (around 300BC), in *The Elements* is accredited with saying: "The whole is greater than the part." Later, someone extended the expression to: "The whole is greater than the sum of the parts." So Pauline and I are '2X' if you consider just the 'parts,' but '25X+' or more as a 'whole' or united force. Together we're stronger and have more influence. It's developing that 'one-ness' that we should be majoring on.

We should all be totally committed to behaviour that builds our marriage. Though we don't want any relationship to sink into the dismal depths of boring routine, there are routine behaviours that increase and enrich 'one-ness' and the relationship.

Interesting positive routine habits pay off. Research has shown that husbands who kiss their wife tenderly every morning before leaving for the day's routine usually live five years longer than those who don't.[69] Kissing husbands have fewer automobile accidents and the research also found that they had 50% less time off work because of illness. And, the bit that will excite all of us passionate kissers is it was discovered they earned 20-30% more than non-kissing husbands.

Sadly, no statistics were available for the benefits of kissing wives. I suppose along with special insurance rates for non-smokers and non-drinkers, there will soon need to be special concessions or policies for male kissers.

We should be totally committed to building a better person called our spouse, our partner in life. Knowing their temperaments and meeting the need of that temperament is vital. Great couples are like a jigsaw. The missing hole, gap, or shape in one piece is filled by the protruding well-rounded section and shape in another. Together the beautiful picture is complete. What is stronger, the gap or the piece that fills? Neither. Each needs the other to both show the whole picture and give strength to the jigsaw.

In marriage it is not that one is better or, one is worse. Essentially, certainly, one isn't good and another one bad. Replace those limiting concepts

---

69 Unidentified newspaper article, reporting on USA University research. Reinforced by: The Kiss Of Health, Susan Krauss Whitborne. Article, July 2012

with 'different.' We are different, uniquely different, and it is in meeting those needs that the relationship can move to a new level.

Tony and Cheryl have slowly learnt to appreciate, understand, and meet the needs of each other's temperament. Clearly Tony saw that Cheryl loved being held, touched gently and massaged. Touching didn't need to lead anywhere. Sensitive massage was therapeutic on its own. Not that it didn't lead somewhere on occasions, but Tony had to watch his motivation. These things were important to whom Cheryl was, not as a necessary and inevitable direction to sex.

Interesting medical research has shown that there is what is cutely called a 'cuddle chemical' or 'love chemical.' Oxytocin facilitates bonding and attraction between humans, being enhanced by the sensation of touch and engendering mutual pleasure and relaxation.

Secreted by the pituitary glands in both genders, the oxytocins are more intense in woman thanks to an interesting synergistic interrelationship with oestrogen/estrogen. The power of touch, sensitive, thoughtful, loving touch and caressing triggers the sense of wellbeing and release of oxytocin. We all both need and can appreciate it.

The Touch Research Institute in the USA[70] discovered that around three, fifteen-minute massages a day on premature babies resulted in a 47% increase in their weight after five days. This research was supported by five other studies worldwide, and is now further confirmed by many hospitals solely specialising in delivery of babies.

A soft therapeutic massage has also been shown to help mums with postpartum (post-natal) depression, general depression, asthma, eating disorders, and psychiatric disorders.

So is Tony just lucky with the effect of touching upon Cheryl? No. This is part of who she is as a woman, but more important who she is as Cheryl. Cheryl likes sensitive touching and that's what Tony has discovered. So Tony does everything he can to meet Cheryl's personal needs and temperament.

---

70 The work of The Touch Research Institute can be easily accessed and assessed on: http://www6.miami.edu/touch-research.

Those loving full-body massages are heaven to her. Once, when their relationship was rocky Tony had little time for them. Now, he finds personal pleasure in meeting her needs expressed through her temperament – who she is as Cheryl.

Tony is careful to exclude the need for eventual sexual intimacy to flow out of his pleasuring massages. Cheryl loves this attention for what it is – attention towards her, non-sexual caring pleasuring.

Cheryl on the other hand knows that a full body massage on Tony does excite and arouse him. She's happy with that, and they both enjoy each other in passionate love making as part of his massage. The key is not meeting each other's 'greeds,' but meeting each other's 'needs.'

Both are determined to meet each other's needs. Self-sacrificing love motivates both Tony and Cheryl.

Cheryl loves shopping; Tony however, is not that keen on the whole concept. Eventually, Tony realises that what is a 'primary' need to Cheryl, may be a 'secondary' need to him. Tony does what he can however to meet her need. As a couple they are evidencing their determination to truly 'love' each other.

In fact, as time goes by Tony starts to enjoy the occasional shopping trip. No, I didn't say he enjoyed shopping, but he enjoys being with Cheryl and seeing and being part of the pleasure such brings her. Tony can always eventually find somewhere quiet for a coffee if necessary and sit and read the paper or a book. And, Cheryl is really happy with this occasional optional male diversion.

Tony, on the other hand, loves fishing, but the thought of slimy, slippery, smelly fish is repugnant to Cheryl. She understands however, that what is even less than a 'secondary' interest to her is 'primary' to Tony. So on occasions Cheryl will accompany Tony out for a day fishing. Those moments when she ties to take a flapping, slippery fish off Tony's line have caused many a good laugh, especially when once she fell out the boat trying to handle the wriggling fish, whilst screaming and giggling.

Does Cheryl essentially like fishing? No, but she likes Tony. When on land Cheryl can enjoy lounging in the sun in her deck chair reading one of her magazines or a book till the next 'slippery critter' gets dragged in.

Both Tony and Cheryl have caught the 'determination' bug. They are sold out to making the relationship work. The desire level is on full throttle and their decision-making capacity to tackle life's difficulties is optimised. Together they are careful to regularly demonstrate their love. Ask yourself, what has fuelled each level? Determination! Raw, unabashed, aggressive determination, that they are going to make their marriage work, drives them.

I could at this point go into complicated analysis of personality temperaments. We all have our favourite way of defining such. There is little point in extensively elaborating temperament types, though below I'll refer in passing very briefly to just one system. Find out your dear one's primary needs, based on who they are, and what their temperament is, then purpose to meet those needs. Please, don't try to change them essentially to what you are or want. That's an instant recipe for disaster.

Many people like the general temperament analysis material that defines people as:

- **Sanguine**

- **Choleric**

- **Melancholy**

- **Phlegmatic.**

Each temperament above has its distinctive features. This is fine, but so often individuals use these absolute definitions as an excuse for their weaknesses or areas they need to work on.

"Oh, that's just the way I am. If you don't like it, you'll just have to like it or lump it." Fine. With an attitude like that, who could tell them anything?

We often don't realise the weakness of how we often present ourselves. A lady was complaining to her husband about the perceived ill manners of a friend who had just left.

"If that woman yawned once whilst I was talking, I'm telling you she yawned ten times."

"Maybe she wasn't yawning, dear," offered her husband. "Possibly she was trying to say something, but couldn't get a word in edgeways."

Certainly, the temperament analysis material will clearly show you your strengths. You should then understand with more empathy why you and others respond the way you/they do, given their distinctive temperament. This shouldn't however, stop us positively addressing the weaknesses we see in ourself.

"Well, if these are my strengths, then these areas are the issues I must work on," referring to not as well-developed areas of our responses. We want to be pro-active with our relationship, or more correctly, with our individual contribution. We want to confront 'us' not him or her.

Lazy relationships slip into entropy. They eventually die. A relationship where both parties are absolutely determined to meet the other's temperament needs shows the same flexibility we had as courting couples. How we did everything to **please** our future spouse back then was amazing. Why have we changed? Revive that 'pleasing' mentality. Fulfil your partner in every way.

Concerning this 'pleasing' issue allow me to make a comment to those of a Christian persuasion. The Apostle Paul in dealing with issues relating to marriage and single relationships makes the following statement in I Corinthians 7: 33 to 34 – viz

*"But a married man has to think about his earthly responsibilities and how to **please his wife**. His interests are divided. In the same way, a woman who is no longer married or has never been married can be devoted to the Lord and holy in body and in spirit. But a married woman has to think about her earthly responsibilities and how to **please her husband**." [New Living Translation: Emphasis ours]*

Don't worry or get lost in the theological explanations about the comparison about singles versus marrieds in this passage. Avoid getting caught up in the theoretical and exegetical wonders of the content. Just observe the responsibility of the marrieds. Clearly our *sole* responsibility expressed in this passage is to *'please'* our spouse – pure and simple.

So in the powerful words of the Nike Company: *Just Do It!*

Five

ONE CAN'T HAVE THEIR CAKE AND EAT IT TOO.

Why not? Why can't you have your cake and eat it too? Why can't you enjoy immensely the current joy in your relationship and then find that literally by doing so your cake has magically multiplied again and there is still more cake to enjoy. Eat and enjoy, otherwise, the cake will get stale. When you are participating together in the rewards of your relationship, you are essentially providing the seed and potential for better days ahead – more cake!

Marginalising your beloved through little jibes in public is 'not' working together. A marriage guidance counsellor offered the following counselling guidance to a woman in her office, after listening to her complain about her marriage, looking directly at her, with the woman's husband sitting alongside her. "Maybe your problem is that you've been waking up grumpy in the morning."

"Oh, no," was the woman's instant reply. "I let him sleep in."

How do we speak about our spouse to others?

Throughout the years, Mia had taken a more active interest in the family business. Together she and Amar had built up a network of eight shops, all highly successful. Life was good, but as family came along, so did the pressures. After each birth, and a few months at home, Mia returned to her side of the business. Her contribution was invaluable, but small tensions were developing at home over housework distribution and child-care.

One USA study in a family-based general magazine found that when both parents were working 55% of couples admitted that they spent too little time with the children. 47% said they did not spend enough time with their spouse. Eventually, nearly 40% found themselves shuffling their children back and forward between divorced partners.

Studies[71] have shown, especially when the children are home (pre-school), that marriages and family life are far more successful when one partner, often the women (but not an absolute), works twenty hours, or less (if they wish to work). The divorce rate heads towards doubling when mothers work full-time as well as running a family – not that it is only her job.

Interesting complimentary research has been done into the effectiveness of the second wage. Does the job truly bring value for hours spent to earn the second wage? The study showed when both partners work full time you will spend a significant amount more on 'different' kinds of food, fast foods, eating out, domestic help inclusive of house cleaning, car washing, gardening maintenance including lawn care and of course child minding.

I am personally staggered at the cost of child minding and after school care. I'm not sure how some families with two, or three children in child-care and after school care can validate the costs against justification of the second wage. In a TV news program dealing with day-care issues and costs that I watched, a woman stated that well over 40% of her wage went to pay child-care alone.

Some suggest that out of the second wage some families, especially with two or more children in child-care, may lose as much as 60 to 70% of its value, when all extra house running costs are considered. Obviously, the highest percentage loss militates against families with several children in day-care, rather than the childless couple.

'Tiredness' kicks in as a reasonably common factor when both partners are working full time. "Oh, I'm too tired to cook. Let's just go out to eat."

---

71   His Needs, Her Needs. Willard F. Harley. Pub: Monarch Publications, Crow borough UK, 1994.

Task completion takes a different slant. How do such couples usually spend the weekend? Doing the housework – what fun! Or, we pay to get the housework done. Oh great, another expense! How do we often relax? Exhausted, not body rejuvenating fun. Rest days are rare, and 'veg out' becomes the norm, instead of doing something constructive and healthy together as a couple and as a family. Then: "Oh no! It's Sunday night already. Back to work on Monday."

Another area that causes me serious concern is how that most Saturdays, for many families, has become completely consumed by sports, cultural events and attending parties. Some families have to take various children to a geographically wide range of sporting venues or other activities, then rush some child off to his/her friend's birthday party (seems to be the norm in younger children up to grade 5/6). I checked with some families and with just two primary school aged children they can attend up to 15 to 20 parties a year between them. What does that do to the household budget having to buy presents all the time, often for children you hardly know, if at all?

Do you remember when you were a child? Did you get to go to 8 to 12 birthday parties a year? Did you actually have a birthday party yourself every year? The answer to the last two questions is 'No!' And, you didn't grow up twisted and socially warped.

Why do we let society dictate to us how we use and distribute our time with our children, conveying we're somehow depriving our kids by not involving them in every sports and music/culture program available, or put demands on our tight budget with often-unnecessary birthday presents, for people we hardly know? You need to take back family time and create quality time.

Refuse to let societal pressure and their selfish expectation control your family. The parents of your child's friend don't really care about you or your values. Take charge of your family. Society mostly is 'amoral,' so you don't need its intrusion, or people's false opinion of you as being 'mean,' as you build a great value-based, character-enhancing family.

When do modern families actually have family time – none interrupted quality time together? Possibly we need to rethink weekends and true family relaxation together.

When one (the second wage earner) works twenty hours or less this whole pressuring cycle on the viability of the second wage is eased, even broken. The extra time can be capitalised by shopping smarter, attending to house and also the family needs. Time is more available for each other and the family. We get better real value out of each dollar earned in the second wage when the second wage spouse is working twenty hours or just less.

I'm not suggesting only the women should reduce to twenty hours or less. On occasions we have all seen very good families where it is Dad who is home for those hours, maybe working from home, whilst the wife is out at work full time. You just have to find what works best for you. Face the difficulties of life with tolerance and grace.

Considering the effect of Mia being away from the home for up to fifty hours a week both Amar and Mia talked about it in a relaxed way. They sensibly agreed together to shift her work commitments to fifteen hours over two days. Their company needed to employ a new administrator, so in his employment he embraced most of Mia's responsibilities. Amar didn't want Mia to work at all, but she enjoyed immensely the involvement and Amar seeing her happy.

Amar and Mia's business continued to grow and so did their family. Soon, three children made a happy family of five. With a firm resolve to build their marriage against any cultural intrusion, whether the culture of the land of their birth, or their Australian culture that they now lived in, they developed a balance of both that was uniquely 'them.'

When the children were old enough to appreciate the trip Amar and Mia took their children for an extended holiday to India. Though of Indian ancestry the children had never seen the land of their parent's birth.

Both Mia and Amar felt that one of the greatest gifts they could pass onto their children was tolerance. They wanted them to appreciate both their Indian heritage and the land of their birth – for them Australia. Before they went on their holiday, they discussed the trip with the children.

"Now, you have to realise that many of our relatives over in India will say to you that only the Indian way is right. Your friends at school here are adamant that only the Australian way is right. You must be tolerant of both points of view. Later in life you will have to make some choices about culture and that will be your decision. Make your choices carefully. Decide what *you* really want, not what your friends want. Your mother and I will support you in what ever way you go in life."

Their trip became four weeks of immense pleasure for the whole family. On occasions, they were totally immersed in the most traditional of Indian culture. Then at times, it was just fun to find the closest McDonalds.

Amar and Mia exemplified their philosophy with their children. Over the years they had faced cultural, financial, and physical difficulties. Mia had been diagnosed with breast cancer, and a mastectomy was required, as part of the successful treatment of the cancer. Oh how cultural opinion tried to intrude then. Amar would have none of it.

For three months, Amar was with his wife in issues relating to her medical treatment at least part of every day. During the surgery and recuperation, he took time off work and never missed a session of chemotherapy with her. Mia came through the ordeal with no recurring problems. Finally, Mia felt she needed and wanted to have breast reconstructive surgery, but Amar said she was every bit as beautiful with or without that breast.

It was his being there, his uncompromising love, his determination to stand by her that brought her through. "Honey, if you want reconstructive surgery that is fine. But, want the reconstruction for 'you,' not for me. I want you to make a decision based on how you feel about yourself, not any per- ceived male need over breasts." Mia giggled at his last statement.

"Oh, I thought I might get a few sizes bigger for you," Mia said humorously.

Continuing the playfulness with Mia, Amar switched to a really strong Indian accent and accompanying shake of the head. "That would look a little odd two different sizes," he chipped in. They both laughed till they had tears rolling down their cheeks.

It is very healthy when we can laugh in the face of difficulties. Laughing with your partner is extremely healthy. Laughing at them can be very danger- ous, but laughing with them is good therapy. Enjoying an interchange like above, has the potential to offend, but shows the depth of emotional security and deepening intimacy Amar and Mia have encouraged their marriage to become, by proactively working on it.

Here, love is going on at many levels. The marriage has blossomed, grown, and matured. The little acorn has become a great oak. The great oak was a testimony to the caring effort by both Mia and by Amar. Its influence on their relatives was effective. The example to their children was priceless.

Mia did proceed with reconstructive surgery, but again Amar was constantly with her. What Amar and Mia taught their children in principles of tolerance, choices and handling life's difficulties they lived before them. They were shining examples of those principles.

They made their choices carefully. They understood the law of consequences is attached to every choice we make. They never left their marriage to suffer with entropy. They kept up the momentum, whether in good or difficult times.

How tolerant are you? Do you convey indifference by the way you respond to people or enthusiasm validating that person? How about your spouse? Are you just tolerating or building them? Listen to the tragic results of just tolerating and/or being critical with children.

In one research reported by *Family Concern* sixty school children were spilt in three groups of twenty, each group with mixed scholastic abilities. They were all given an arithmetic test every day for five days.

One group was constantly praised over the previous results. Another group was criticised every day over the previous results. The final group was simply ignored every day.

The 'praised' group radically improved. The 'criticised' group marginally improved, whilst the 'ignored' group showed little improvement at all.

Just tolerating a person is not healthy. Build them up with praise and affirmation. Own your responsibility for your partner's growth.

Six

YOU'VE MADE YOUR BED, NOW LIE IN IT.

Isn't that ridiculous? Does this imply we will never be able to change, even if we made some bad choices earlier in life? Attack this fatalistic statement head on. Under this destructive life-view we will never be able to address issues within a changing relationship.

With such a disabling attitude as our guide self-esteem will always be low, because the saying implies we can't undo things we've done. How mind controlling is that? Refuse to lie down. Refuse to have a 'messy bed.' Get up make your bed and go out and conquer the day. Take your life and your relationship to a new level.

Don't pass your problems onto your spouse. Whilst on their honeymoon in a brilliant sunny climate, with whitewashed pristine white buildings, with brilliant red bougainvillea on the walls, blue-glazed tiled roofs and brilliant, shimmering aquamarine sea, a newly married young woman cast a disapproving eye towards her husband of three days.

"That's the third time you've been back in the shop for more butterscotch flavoured ice-cream and cake, John," she said caustically. "Doesn't it embarrass you at all?"

"Why should it?" responded the young man with a glint in his eye, and ice cream on the corner of his mouth and tip of his nose. "I just keep telling the ice-cream man I'm getting the cake and ice-cream for you."

Whilst it is very difficult to have definitive lists of things that cause poor self-esteem strong indicators emerge from reliable research. In the Australian Government Parliamentary Report *To Have And To Hold*,[72] the report included well-documented research on the impact of marital breakdown on the lives of family members. To quote from the report: "For adults, a stable, happy marriage is the best protector against illness and premature death, and for children, such marriage is the best source of emotional stability and good physical health."

The report went on to indicate that adults and children are at increased risk of mental and physical problems resulting from marital distress. There is conclusive evidence to show that marriage is a 'healthy environment' associated with lower mortality and morbidity. And there is strong evidence that the process of divorce leaves men, women, and children vulnerable to ill heath, not the least its effect upon their self-esteem.

In an Australian Institute of Family Studies[73] article *Marital Conflict And Adolescents*; certain teenagers were identified as 'Becoming Emotional' and 'Withdrawing.' The research went on to say: "Some of the responses in the 'Becoming Emotional' and 'Withdrawing' categories suggested that marital conflict can be quite stressful for adolescents, and may lead to them feeling quite negative, not only about their parents, but about themselves."

Tragically teenagers have suicided over such pressures. What do we want for our children? Surely nothing but the best. Then work on building a great relationship that builds a great family.

Contessa continued to grow in self-esteem as Graham poured self-sacrificing love into her system. They both noticed that when she was feeling low for natural or unusual reasons her self-esteem dropped. Pre-menstrual tension

---

72 To Have And To Hold: Parliamentary Committee Report. 'Strategies To Strengthen Marriage And Relationships (June 1998). Chairperson: Kevin Andrews. Parliamentary Paper: 95/1998; Tabled in Australian Parliament: 22 June 1998.
73 The Relation Of Parental Marital Status And Perceived Family Conflict To Adjustment In White Adolescents. The Australian Institutes of Family Studies. Edwards. June 1987.

was often difficult for Contessa. Sadly, during those times Contessa felt less of herself than was healthy for her overall opinion of herself. Graham noticed the trend and moved in with extra support and encouragement during those critical days each month.

Graham understood his determination to help and stand with Contessa would determine the outcome and feeling she had about herself.

Together with Contessa Graham attended a specialist women's clinic that helped her with her Pre-menstrual tension issues. He was there for her. "No honey, this is our problem together, not yours alone," Graham assured her. Over time, her system settled down. This was further aided with the addition of natural supplements, and Graham's sensitivity during difficult days.

Few of us are built without the need for someone else in our life, that 'essential other,' to help us ultimately reach our full potential. That is the very vulnerability of a relationship. Someone can know us so well, be so close to us that at times we can feel exposed, almost naked emotionally in their presence. Our spouse can either protect our weaknesses or expose them, if not for all to see (which is an unforgivable cruelness), then for us to gaze in a mirror of self with a frightened heart, that we falsely think reflects ugliness.

It had originally been at Graham's encouragement that Contessa had joined the Lord Mayor's Committee that was involved in organising so many civic projects. Over the years, and with the passage of several different Lord Mayors Contessa became the public face and chairperson of this group. Her self-esteem was developing into strength.

Then the inevitable happened. Before one committee meeting a fellow committee member burst into tears. Her daughter, Jasmine, had been in a live-in situation with her boyfriend and had been viciously raped as he angrily terminated their relationship. It had been Jasmine's mother that had called the police after finding her daughter distraught, huddled in a corner of the lounge room of her flat in a foetal position two days after the rape.

The police could do very little, despite their sensitive handling of the situation, because of the complete lack of a hospital or medical verification and corroborating evidence. Of concern to the police had been her live-in status with the boyfriend and the fact that Jasmine wouldn't eventually press charges, talk about the situation and attack with the police, or attend a medical check. She eventually even refused to talk to her mother about it.

"What am I going to do? She's so withdrawn. Jasmine won't go out. She's stopped working. She's…" and Helen burst into tears again. Contessa comforted Helen and bit the bullet. Over the next two weeks, meeting every two days with Jasmine, Contessa brought life, confidence, and self-esteem back to her, by personally sharing privately with Jasmine her own heart-rending struggle with similar pressures. Jasmine's life was back to normal in a few weeks.

In one Mayoral Committee meeting Contessa raised the issue of starting a self-help group for abuse victims. Tentatively, very tentatively because of the male dominance and staid thinkers, the city council agreed. Within a year the six-part workshop course had become a major contributor to helping countless victims of violence, rape and self-defeating poor self-esteem.

Over years the program became so successful that other councils, around the country, were asking for help as they implemented the model of operation and program Contessa had developed. She called her program 'SELF' [Sensibly Evaluating Life's Feelings]. It powerfully met the needs of those attending.

Contessa began to travel throughout the country, running seminars and assisting setting up similar self-help groups. What was the worst in Contessa's life possessed the seeds to become her best. She eventually triumphed over her dreadful experiences and their negative impact on her self-esteem.

Graham did nothing but encourage her. In every six-week course in her own local area, that Contessa ran, Graham would come along and share how males can support the process. Men were specifically invited to that session. Graham was so proud of Contessa. A changing, maturing relationship became a journey to both Graham and Contessa, not a single event.

Once Momma tried to silence Contessa's public work. "Nice girls don't talk about those things. You, be a good girl. No do it." Graham had never seen Contessa respond so quickly.

"Momma, we love you dearly. But, you're wrong – dead wrong! If you had been more open about it, I would have been able to come to you as a young girl and a teenager. However, you weren't. So I suffered alone. Understand this, I'm going to make sure other girls don't suffer alone." Graham almost stood up, applauded and cheered. However, he didn't. Graham didn't want to incur Momma's wrath, as he loved her cooking too much. Momma, much to Graham's amusement, was now 'just' tolerating him.

On the way home Graham told Contessa how proud he was of what she had just done. "You were brilliant. You should have seen Momma's mouth. Wide open catching flies." Graham roared laughing. Contessa dug him in the ribs playfully. Importantly they still had a great playful relationship. There is something special about a couple that can still be as playful as they were in their courting days – something very special.

True love, genuine love was building strong self-esteem. Strong self-esteem was building a warm, confident marriage. Both Graham and Contessa were enjoying the journey. Eventually, Contessa would successfully run for public office as a councillor. Later Contessa would become Mayoress – the first Mayoress in her city's history. Oh how Momma was proud of this.

"Contessa my girl. Always knew she would do well." Momma was proud for herself, not her daughter, because of all the attention her daughter's position brought her. How sad. Tragically, Momma had not been supportive of Contessa as a young girl or as a grown woman.

When we know who we are, when we've dealt with the junk in our life we can reach out to others with strength to make them feel and look good. That really builds relationship. Such was Contessa's gift to others.

Tragically, when we don't know who we are (like Momma), and we haven't effectively dealt with the hurt and pains from the past the way we tend to reach out to others is to make them make us look and feel good. And that my friend is too high a price in any relationship and such actions may 'potentially' destroy the relationship or deform it.

Contessa and Graham brought the Prince and the Princess out of each other. They developed the Beauty not the Beast. They were 'determined' not to let entropy touch their relationship. They were proactive in keeping their marriage alive, hot, passionate, fun, romantic and all that fulfils not destroys.

Progressively Contessa's self-esteem grew in a healthy way. Understand that this boosting and growth is not a five-minute-wonder. Positive self-esteem must be part of our philosophy of building a better person, called your spouse.

Many of you would have heard of Tony Campolo. What an outstanding, though often controversial and thought provoking speaker he is. Tony Campolo's wife Peggy chose to be at home with the children when they were younger and growing up. It was a deliberate, powerful and purposeful choice. Because of Tony's very high academic position and profile Peggy often had to attend with Tony fairly 'high-brow' University, Academic and Government functions.

Sure enough some insecure professional woman would mark Peggy out, and knowing she was at home with the children, sidle up to her and ask: "And what is it that you do my dear?" full well knowing, as if being at home with precious children was somehow a second rate job.

As Tony tells it, Peggy's answer was not just good; it was brilliant. Looking them square in the eyes she is reported as saying:

"I am socializing two homo sapiens into the dominant values of the Judeo-Christian tradition in order that they might be instruments for the transformation of the social order into the telelogically prescribed Utopia inherent in the eschaton."[74]

[Or, if you want her comment in brief she's saying: I'm raising my two children in God's plan for their lives to effectively live in today's society].

At which point Peggy then looked directly at them and said: "And, what is it that you do my dear?"

"Oh, I'm just a doctor..." they offered embarrassed. Classic. I love it. Let's all pick up our enthusiasm for being a unique person.

Know who you are and don't let any person set the agenda of your life. Contessa eventually put her mother in her place. Contessa needed to find out what was best for Contessa, not her mother.

---

74 The Power Delusion. Anthony Campolo. Victor Books, 1984, pp. 31.

In the United States Wallerstein and Blakeslee[75] interviewed fifty happy couples, with children. The average length of marriage was twenty-one years, and they were on average forty-eight years old.

The Wallerstein, Blakeslee analysis showed the following characteristics of the happy couples: "respect, integrity, friendship, trust and feeling cherished; a view of their spouse as special in some important way and someone whose company they still enjoy; and the sense that creating *their marriage and family* have been their *major commitment and their greatest achievement*." [Emphasis ours]

Question: Do you think the above listing builds or destroys self-esteem? I think you don't need more than a second to respond to that. Well, if such actions work for them then be smart. Why reinvent the wheel? Copy those who have made good their marriage.

On February 10th 2014, at 85 years of age the well-known child star, Shirley Temple Black, died. Though famous for her many brilliant movies as a child-star, her starring with famous Hollywood names, and later her role as a diplomat and ambassador for the USA, it is interesting to hear her comment about her important 'roles' in life.

Shirley Temple Black is quoted by journalists from her speech given at her 'Lifetime Achievement Award' at the Screen Actors Guild, in 2006: "But she also said that evening that her greatest roles were as a wife, mother and grandmother, finally saying: There's nothing like real love. Nothing."[76]

Let her illuminating comments and challenge about the importance of marriage and family inspire us.

---

75 The Good Marriage: How And Why Love Lasts. Judith Wallerstein, Sandra Blakeslee. Pub: Grand Central Publishing. 1996.
76 The Daily Telegraph (Sydney), Wednesday, February 12th, 2014, pp. 18, 19.

Seven

Two wrongs don't make a right.

We have to convert our wrongs into rights. The worst things that happen to us can become the seeds of our destiny and change opportunities in our life, if we are courageous enough to see failure, wrongs or mistakes as the flip side of learning something good.

Let's learn to grow from our mistakes. One couple received, among other things, a toaster capable of taking four slices of bread for a wedding present. Soon after the honeymoon they tried out the toaster. Almost immediately smoke billowed out of the wedding present. "Switch it off. Get the owner's manual," called out the husband.

"I can't find it anywhere!" she cried, searching through the box.

"Oops!" came a voice from deep inside the smoke-filled kitchen. The smoke alarm was making a high-pitched piercing shrieking noise. "Well, the two pieces of toast are fine, but the owner's manual is a little on the burnt side," yelled the husband above the noise of the alarm.

If we are concerned with and proposing 'confrontational marriage,' then things that go wrong need to be and can be confronted. I understand that may take incredible resolve and courage. Aren't we man enough, woman enough to do it? Now, I again repeat, and will continue to repeat till it's ingrained in our psyche, 'confrontational marriage' is not confronting our spouse, but confronting ourself.

When something isn't working, causing arguments, creating friction then right there you will find opportunity to grow. We should be smart enough to confront ourself. I might tell myself off and say: "Ivan, don't be so stupid and insecure. This doesn't work. If I can change the way I approach it, it may change the outcome."

Directly confronting conflict management methods, instead of avoiding issues, is often central to a maturing relationship.

Over time Clyde and Chris have changed the way they approach differences. The Round Table has not only become a different way of doing things, but their positive action has forced them personally to make changes.

Now many years after they instituted the tradition, their Round Table is more a friend, more a place where they sit and chat. Long ago the kitchen and its table ceased to be a place where they settled World War III.

Both Chris and Clyde confronted their own actions instead of their spouse's. Chris is now far more confident and relaxed to share her opinion and persist with sensible discussion. Clyde has relaxed, calmed down and now can discuss anything in a calm voice. He no longer sees the need to rant, rave, walk around using an ever-increasing loud voice, arm gestures and threaten with finger pointing.

Chris thought it was hilarious and an interesting illustration of change that recently when they were over at his parent's house at a family barbeque that all the family were in full swing with their loud conversations and physically moving in on one another. Yet, Clyde was not involved.

But, where was Clyde? Turning over the meat on the barbeque with Chris, Clyde watched the interactions. Clyde refused to participate in the mayhem.

"Just look at them," Clyde said pointing over his shoulder, with his meat tongs, to his eldest brother and his Dad going head to head. "I used to be like that. Scary wasn't it?"

Chris giggled but added: "We've come a long way haven't we King Arthur?" Clyde looked at her and gave her a kiss on the forehead. "Sure have Lady Guinevere, sure have."

Right then their tranquil intimate moment was shattered by Jake, Clyde's older brother yelling. "Clyde, you agree with me about the car, don't you? Come here and tell Dad."

"No Jake. If you're going to yell at Dad like that, showing him no respect, I'm not entering in. Why don't you and Dad come over here, sit down and have a chat in a normal voice? I refuse to raise my voice or physically get in either your or Dad's face or personal space. Now come and sit down and talk quietly."

Jake had his mouth wide open, speechless. He had just been properly told off by his younger brother in a tone of voice that was pleasant and at several decibels below his contribution.

Both Jake and their Dad obediently came and sat down like two well trained chastened puppies. For nearly twenty minutes, before lunch was ready, everybody chatted about whatever. When anybody slipped back into shouting or a loud voice Clyde would say. "Come on there's no need to raise your voice. Your point is really appreciated for its intelligence not its volume."

Eventually, everyone, all ten adults were sitting around having a 'normal' conversation. Chris could not believe it. She had never seen them all so relaxed and the volume of conversation so pleasant.

As they drove home Chris looked across at Clyde. "Well King Arthur, are you extending the Round Table?" They both laughed, but agreed the day had been their most pleasurable visit to his parent's home that they could remember.

Chris patted Clyde's leg. "You know Chantel came to me afterwards and said to tell you 'thank you.' This was the first time Chantel had every heard Jake have a family conversation about anything at a sensible volume level and without needing to appear aggressive."

Determination was the central motivation of Clyde and Chris. They had converted their misused negative energy into life-injecting, relationship-building energy. Their marriage and their relationship grew with time. Nothing was left to chance. They refused to let their love dissipate and slowly slip away. Constructively they built an ever-stronger foundation for more happy years to come.

Chris and Clyde discovered a successful conflict management technique. The Round Table was creatively their invention. Interestingly their invention worked. Many people incorrectly feel they need to eliminate all conflict from their life, thinking 'all conflict is wrong.'

Do you realise that is not helpful? What you really need to do is manage conflict constructively, not destructively. Refocus its energy from negative to positive.

Therapists often use what is called: 'The Principle Of Redefinition' as a useful tool of conflict management. As an illustration let us say that a woman feels her husband is not being affectionate enough outside the bedroom.

When he gets home from work, as he walks in the kitchen, the husband puts a kiss on the nap of his wife's neck, gives her shoulders a squeeze and says: "Hi honey. Love you. How was your day? How can I help?"

Still concentrating on putting the third vegetable on the dinner plates and tending to the meat she says in a harsh tone of voice: "We've got to talk." Now, hubby knows she's been upset about something for a couple of days. Husbands are smart that way, though they often don't know the cause of the tension.

Being even smarter, by not wanting to involve the children who are already in the kitchen checking out dinner he says: "Honey, I know something is bothering you, but now is not the right time to discuss it. After dinner, I'll do all the washing up whilst you get the kids started with their homework in their bedrooms. Then, we can have a coffee in peace on the back terrace and chat."

One communicator developing successful marriage principles says that: "Most men forget what is the irritation in the marriage, or an issue raised, after 24 hours. The trouble is, most women don't raise it for 48 hours."

In the illustration above the husband above hasn't got a clue what the issue is, though he knows 'something' is a problem. But, clearly the wife has been brooding on it for a while. Not a healthy combination.

It is important to recognise you need two essential environments to settle a difference. Firstly, you need 'privacy' and secondly, you need 'time.' This couple have neither of these right now. Try not, as much as possible, to attempt to settle a disagreement or manage your conflict:

- *Just before you go out.*

- *Just before a meal.*

- *Just before you go to bed.*

- *Set special time aside.*

Later, after the washing up was done and the children are busily doing their homework in their rooms the couple relax with their coffees. Sitting out on the back terrace the husband asks his wife what is wrong.

"Well, **I** just don't think there's enough affection outside the bedroom," she blurts out, still with a little tension in her voice.

Now in the Principle Of Redefinition each person gets to define or more correctly redefine what they have just heard.

The husband chooses to ignore the slight tone in her voice and might say: "Let **me** see if **I** have this right. Is it suggested **I'm** not affectionate enough?" Was she saying that? Not really. He has got some of the words right, but he's got them in a different sentence. It's like the expression: 'I understood every word you said, but not a single sentence!'

Now she redefines: "No honey. **I** mustn't have explained it well enough."

The use of personal inclusive pronouns – eg: '**I**,' '**me**,' '**my**,' '**mine**' etc are absolutely vital to the process. I have put each use in bold type, so you can see how each stands out in the flow of the dialogue. Use of the accusative 'you' will ruin the flow and mostly cause the discussion to descend into unhealthy recriminations.

For example, how do you think he would have responded if she had said: "No, weren't you listening you dummy!" – World War III here we come. If 'you' is used as a word it is only ever used either in praise or to ask a question.

She continues. "Let me see if **I** can explain it better. **I** just think that sometimes outside the bedroom there's not enough affection."

Now if he got upset at that, he's not really trying, as she's not criticising, but explaining things from her point of view, from her perspective.

So, he now redefines again. "Let, **me** see if **I've** got it this time." Notice he is only using the personal inclusive pronouns, never the accusative 'you.' This is very important.

"Can **I** ask a question sweetheart?"

"Sure Honey."

"Is the amount of affection inside the bedroom good enough?"

"Oh yes," she says. "You're sensitive to **my** needs, romantic, wonderful. Thank you."

"Thank goodness for that he says," playfully pretending to sweep sweat off his brow. They both laugh. "So you're saying at times it appears that **I'm** not sensitive enough on the non-sexual side of the bedroom door, like Ivan and Pauline talk about the two sides of the bedroom door?"

The discussion and redefining simply goes from one to the other continually redefining each other's words till one can say: "That's it. That's what **I'm** talking about honey."

This simple technique has as its fundamental core that nobody is trying to win. Nobody is trying to score points. The technique is based on the ancient relationship-enriching statement of Francis of Assisi: "Seek first to understand before being understood."

Of course, the modern motivation, and leadership gurus want to rebadge it as 'Win-Win' or possibly incorrectly 'Synergy' method, without honouring Francis of Assisi. Steven Covey in *The 7 Habits Of Highly Effective People*[77] actually refers to Assisi's words renaming them as his 5th Habit in his book, without Francis of Assisi being once recognised. But, in all honesty I suppose it would be a bit difficult to split any royalties with Assisi. The 25 pages he gives to developing the concept are well worth the read.

---

77 Stephen Covey, The 7 Habits Of Highly Effective People. The Business Library (Melbourne), 1997 edition. Habit No 7 dealt with on pp 235-260.

In conclusion of the illustration about the above couple, the husband may be sitting there thinking: "But, I think I am affectionate enough outside the bedroom." Then, he remembers what the last six weeks has been like for his wife.

Nearly six weeks ago his wife's mother was killed in a tragic car accident. A month ago her brother was diagnosed with a virile form of cancer and has been hospitalised because of being so ill for the last three weeks. Currently he is undergoing invasive chemotherapy, and is very sick from the extended treatment.

Last week their youngest son just six years of age fell off his skateboard and dislocated his shoulder and was overnight in hospital and still nurses a very sore shoulder supported in a sling, that causes sleep deprivation and difficulties.

Maybe, the husband may not be lacking in attention outside the bedroom. It may just be that his wife essentially needs more hugs at this time in her life and is not expressing her needs as well as she could. We have to learn to honestly and non-defensively check out what is happening and 'why' the situation is happening. Then, we can appropriately respond.

Clyde and Chris have learned this 'understanding' lesson well. As a result, their marriage has blossomed.

The professional counsellor friend of Clyde had also suggested another conflict management technique. The technique is called 'Replacement Therapy.' Often, we are looking for absolutes, when we in actual fact should be changing or replacing our concepts.

For example replace right, wrong or better, worse with the concept and word 'different.' We are always trying to figure out who is right or wrong, better, or worse. Drop it. Replace each area with the liberating concept of different. Different is good.

Replace the square boxing ring concept with the round boxing ring concept. Often, when our partner holds particular views we feel we must find an opposing corner and almost cry out: "Someone hand me the gloves." Why do we always have to defend a corner, always opposing?

Try thinking about a round boxing ring. "Hey, honey I didn't realise this was so important to you. I'm sorry I missed the cue. Let's work on this together." We're both on the same side of the ring. And, we're not boxing.

Square boxing rings have corners to defend. Round boxing rings have no corners to defend. Smart hey!

We don't always have to have a different opinion. Try to get on the same side. Sort through your differences on key issues. Don't major on minors. You don't always need to oppose.

Replace 'demand' with 'prefer.'

Replace concept of 'confrontation' with 'carefrontation.' You don't need to confront everything. The word 'confront, conflict' etc have their roots in the Latin word 'fligere,' which mean 'to strike together, to beat down,' or by a wider implication 'to light a fire,' hence conflagration. The term's origin is negative to its roots.

'Carefrontation' is a cute word, developed by David Augsburger.[78] Using the term means I care enough about you, your opinion, our relationship, the topic, and my own opinion to resolve this harmoniously together.

Finally replace 'I can't' with 'I'm going to try.' These interesting replacement therapy techniques will help you build a strong relationship.

When we throw our whole determination behind these changes in thinking, things start to happen. Be patient with yourself as well as your spouse. Many changes take time.

See determination as a friend and not a process equivalent to chewing on bricks.

---

78 Caring Enough To Confront. David Augsburger, Pub: Regal Books, Ventura, 1986.

Eight

YOU MUST WEAR CLEAN UNDERWEAR; IN CASE YOU GET RUN OVER BY A BUS.

Oh, how fatalistic some of the old statements were. Can you remember your mother or grandmother saying the above to you? I can. How on earth can we build a fantastic life-injecting relationship when we are always expecting the worst?

A couple in an argument started using ridiculing demeaning statements. "I should have taken my mother's advice and never married you! Oh, how she tried to stop me," yelled the wife.

"Good grief," pleaded the husband. "How I've misjudged that woman."

Expect the best, not the worst. Expect the best, not the 'bus.'

Ladies, put clean pretty, feminine, intimate underwear on, because you want to feel good about yourself, pretty and special – because you are. Don't think 'buses,' think beauty.

Guys wear clean underwear because you need to change them!

Seriously, we need to confront negative views of life that can, like some insidious cancer, affect every part of our life, thinking, and relationships in general. Instead of showing positive 'determination', many are specialist in 'defensiveness.' They are not expecting the best they are living the worst. Here comes the bus!

What is so hard about believing for the best?

Ted and Beverly never quite mastered this principle. Beverly came from a home where in her extended family every marriage had broken up before they turned forty-five years of age, inclusive of her parents. This underlying, gnawing, ever-present mental fact played on the stability of her thinking.

Behaviour was no better for Ted. He listened too much to the guys at the gym, and the pub. "Everybody has a bit on the side mate" (Though this is totally untrue). "What are you worried about? All you got to worry about is Beverly doesn't find out. Get smart."

Get smart about what? That you give into fatalistic attitudes and mentally controlling, habitually destructive consuming behaviours? Is Ted smart listening to mates 'hell-bent' on giving destructive advice?

Instead of confronting themselves, Ted and Beverly are confronting each other.

Beverly's fellow airhostesses weren't helpful either. "Marriage who needs it? Play the field girl. It's more interesting. Marriage is a bit like a hot bath. Once you get used to it, it's not so hot." Off walked 'Miss Expert,' that was already into her third marriage and even that was virtually over.

Trying to inject humour into a painful sore for Beverly, another close fellow airhostess friend Rebecca, who was not married, spoke up.

"I've never married, as you all know. I don't see the need. You see I just figured that I'd keep three pets, which fulfil all the purposes of a husband. You know I have my dog Brutus, well he growls every morning. My pet parrot, Percy, swears all afternoon and I have a cat, Caesar who comes home very late at night, or early morning. Why would I need a husband?" Rebecca walked off down the isle to deliver drinks to the passengers, with a deliberate wiggle of her backside before she parted the curtain to the passengers. Everyone laughed.

Tragically for Ted and Beverly they were now expecting their marriage to fail. It was only a matter of who would blow the whistle for full time first. Ted wasn't looking for commitment, so his one-night stands had become a regular excuse for the decreasing sexual expression in marriage. He started drinking to excess. In these drunken moods Ted not only became verbally, but physically abusive. One night he hit Beverly hard. The die was cast in her mind – she wanted out.

Beverly eventually succumbed to the wily charms of Harry, even though he was married, who as a pilot regularly flew the trans-Pacific route with her. All the airhostesses knew what he was like, but that didn't stop him bedding most of them, including Beverly. For a while, she was the flavour of the month.

Ted and Beverly had lost the desire, the positive decision-making, and the demonstration of love in their marriage. Both of them had not totally lost and undervalued determination. Yet, it was the wrong sort of determination. Theirs was not the sort of determination to keep the marriage alive. As the relationship deteriorated to arguing and heated verbal and sometimes physical abuse of each other they seemed to be totally determined to do one thing – end their marriage.

It was Beverly who moved out, relocating herself to a flat with a fellow stewardess. Seeing Ted and Beverly had kept separate bank accounts, and rented a fully furnished flat, they just called everything square, after evenly dividing the white goods, other electrical products and personal household items. Sadly, they became another statistic. Ted took over the flat lease obligations, when it came time to renew it.

How tragic that love so passionate can end up as hatred so violent – in the same couple. They destructively transferred the initial energy of love into the soul-destroying criticism of bitterness. Eventually, hatred seethed through both of them. Had they created hatred? No just transferred the same energy they once had for loving into far less constructive behaviours. Don't forget energy can transform from one state to another.

Over the last year of their marriage they had left relationship-building out of their thinking, let alone any actions. Survival had been their only goal. Another couple hit the dust. Ted and Beverly didn't keep their relationship either moving or creative. Entropy set it. Then their relationship left to itself began to self-destruct.

An interesting study in the UK[79] found that 44% of all domestic violence occurs under the influence of alcohol. As much as Ted tried to redeem his

---

79   Health First: An Evidence-based Alcohol Strategy For The UK. University of Starling. 2013.

way out of his disgraceful attack on Beverly, by bringing her flowers, he hadn't woken up to one pertinent fact. Sorry is more than flowers. Sorry is changing our behaviour.

A study in Greece[80] (urban & rural) showed 67% of domestic violence victims are married and educated. There's sometimes sadly an attitude around that all studies show only the uneducated, lower socio-economic, and de facto groupings act and suffer this way.

Mind you, it needs to be understood that de facto relationships are not as high in Greece generally or rural Greece in particular. However, some studies in the more urbanised Western cities clearly do sadly show de facto violence to be much higher by percentage than in married relationships.

Over half the women surveyed, in the Greek study indicated they had been physically and/or psychologically abused. Sadly for centuries it has been tolerated as an unspoken cultural issue. The sickening statistics showed 81% of culprits were husbands.

Yet, a man or woman need never raise their hand to their spouse/partner to be an abuser. Verbal and psychological abuse is just as damaging. Some suggest over time psychological abuse can have a far worse effect as the behaviour often cripples the tender spirit, self-esteem, and dreams of the victim.

As previously indicated, have you ever wondered how that love so potential, can end up to be so empty and soul destroying, in the same couple? What has happened? Where did this hatred, shallowness, and such disrespect for another precious human being come from? How was this hatred created? It wasn't.

Energy isn't created or destroyed, but it is transferred from one form to another. What are we transferring?

Sadly abusers transfer once passionate love, and genuine desire into something so debasing we're all horrified.

Unless individuals learn to control anger and aggression it will consume them. Anger is everybody's problem. Every 1.5 to 2 seconds a serious crime is committed in the USA; much anger based.

---

80 Violence begins at home. Le Monde diplomatique. Ignacio Ramonet. 2013.

In the UK, with a much smaller population size than the USA, researchers state a serious crime occurring every 5 seconds.[81] Many crimes are executed out of anger, with people feeling angry about their position in life, as if that justifies them.

Anger will also negatively affect the health of an individual, particularly affecting the immune system. Isn't it an appalling fact that Domestic Violence is the No.1 health problem for women in the Western World?[82] If that's the 'civilised world' I would hate to know what 'uncivilised' would be.

If you are really serious about dealing with anger and you know such is an issue with you (you are being brutally honest with yourself), then let me be the first to congratulate you for being that open. Secondly, I recommend you sign up for an 'Anger Management Class' that will be conducted somewhere in your area.

Be brave. Don't get embarrassed, just deal with your anger.

Conclusion To Choices And Destiny & Final Thoughts.

We never seem to have enough time. We must not however give into the re-lationship-destroying pronouncement: "When, we've got time we'll get round to it." At the point of writing this book our children are all over forty years of age. Now they are all married with their own children. Where did the time go? We are so grateful we never said: "When we've got enough time we'll have a great family." We took a proactive approach to marriage and family life. You've always got time.

Don't ask time where it's gone, tell it where to go. Prioritise marital and family time separately and together.

Walking up the beach from our UK hotel on the west coast, whilst travel-ling overseas on speaking engagements with Pauline, the sun was beginning its brilliant colour-creating descent. The setting was so restful. Yes, we had

---

81 Mail Online. Crime Committed Every Five Seconds. Aug. 2013.
82 Violence Against Women: An Urgent Public Health Priority. Claudia Garcia-Moreno & Charlotte Watts. World Health Organisation. *Bulletin of the World Health Organization* 2011; 89:2-2. doi: 10.2471/BLT.10.085217.

a thousands things to do. However, we've always got time to invest in each other.

Two other couples from our hotel are nearby taking in the beauty of the close of a cloudless June day. They were also enjoying together a particularly beautiful evening.

A young couple, three years married are sitting arms around each other's waists, oblivious to the world. They exude love. We stop to talk and admire their first-born. "Charlotte," they proudly share.

We move on to find an aged couple, she in a wheelchair, he seated on a seat next to her, sitting watching the soft gentle small waves just flopping on the beach, the circling, shrieking gulls, the liquid gold, now spreading over an aquamarine near still ocean free of significant wave swells. Ripples of gold seem to spread from a sun just kissing the horizon.

We had talked with Henry and Anna in the hotel. Celebrating their fiftieth wedding anniversary they have come like young lovers, wheelchair or no wheelchair, to their favourite holiday beach town, where they had honeymooned fifty years ago.

Age may have slowed their bodies, but not their hearts. We wave, they respond back. Snuggled up into each other, it would be intrusive to stop to chat.

Interestingly, they make just one shadow behind them. Two have become one. As we stroll in the warm summer breeze, the soft lapping sound of the waves, the friendly ever food-hungry cry of the circling white gulls, and the colour transforming surface of the water and impending night all speak of peace and tranquillity. Romance is in the air for everyone.

Looking back along the beach, beside many others enjoying its stunning beauty that night, are two special couples. Will Charlotte's parents reach the wondrous state of blissful marriage of Anna and Henry? Who will know? If they have continuing time for each other like they do tonight, there's a very strong chance they will make it.

Through this book, you have met several couples. Some have kept their marriage alive, working through the tough times. Sadly, some couples haven't survived.

In the *Introduction* Section, we talked of a 4D relationship. Throughout the four Sections we have highlighted each of the contributing helpful 'D's' to a positive relationship, and the couples you have met have wrestled with each factor. Some have won. Some have lost. Such is life.

By way of review and conclusion, let us examine the 4D's in the following table that we have raised, and what areas they address.

Give your marriage a check-up from the neck-up. No matter how long you have been married, have you kept the desire, the passion, fun, and romance alive? You have to work on it. This is keeping the relationship moving, refusing to let the marriage stall.

In realising the utter importance of these life-injecting, relationship-maintaining factors, we then move onto the decision stage. We make a conscious decision, come what may, to keep the desire stage and marriage alive. We are conscious of the 'bulls,' but we joyfully keep running together.

Figure 3.
Review Of Our Model Of Effective Marriage

KEY FACTOR IN MARRIAGE	ADDRESSING WHAT ISSUES	AFFECTING WHAT AREAS
SEC. 1: DESIRE SIDE OF THE RELATIONSHIP	Motivational Side Of The Marriage	Maintaining Passion, Desire, Fun & Romance
SEC. 2: DECISION SIDE OF THE RELATIONSHIP	Cognitive Side Of The Marriage	Resolving Commitment, Working Through Issues
SEC. 3: DEMONSTRATION SIDE OF THE RELATIONSHIP	Emotional Side Of The Marriage	Deepening Intimacy Demonstrating Love At Every Level
SEC. 4: DETERMINATION SIDE OF THE RELATIONSHIP	Life-Choices Side Of The Marriage	Expressing Our Determination To Be Proactive And Not Reactive

From that resolve and commitment in the second stage we flow into the third stage or phase. Here, intimacy is being further developed, and the emotional responses are kept buoyantly alive. We are now deliberately demonstrating the commitment of the Decision Stage. Emotional security reigns.

Finally, we understand the power of choices that must pervade every dimension and set our mind, spirit, energy, and determination to choose life, not death in our relationship. May we all have what it takes to not only make a go of it, but to make a go of marriage in style.

So in *'Marital Physics'* we suggest a great relationship may possibly be able to be brought down to a formula. Let's think of it as:

Figure 4.
OUR MODEL AS A FORMULA

$$\frac{\text{DESIRE} \ + \ \text{DECISION} \ + \ \text{DEMONSTRATION}}{\text{DETERMINATION}}$$

On the beach, that day there was three couples taking our attention. – Charlotte's Mum and Dad, Henry and Anna, Pauline, and I. Pauline and I have already made a conscious decision where we want to end up – just as happily married well over fifty years (nearly there) as we were when we first said 'I do."

Henry and Anna have made it. It remains to be seen if Charlotte's Mum and Dad will. If they keep the desire side of love alive like we saw in them on the beach, they have a good chance. Then, adding to desire a resolute decision to make their relationship work through the tough times, they will be able to add to their progress in demonstration of the deepening intimacy. Finally, their positive determination will be necessary. Their choices have been cast. They are going to succeed. Here, we write the script of our destiny – yours too, we hope.

What sort of a destiny do you want? I want to write a positive destiny with the 'Princess' by my side. I want to achieve things together, I, or we, could never achieve alone.

You do have a choice, but the soul-destroying alternates to Desire, Decision, Demonstration, and Determination is not all that palatable. Consider the highly negative alternate 4D's, attempting to replace the positive dimensions and subvert your marriage:

Figure 5.
YOUR OPTION OF CHOICES

KEY POSITIVE LIFE-INJECTING CORRECT 4D RESPONSES	ADDRESSING WHAT ISSUE	KEY NEGATIVE SOUL-DESTROYING OPPOSITE 4D RESPONSES
DESIRE	MOTIVATIONAL SIDE OF THE MARRIAGE	DISINTEREST
DECISION	COGNITIVE SIDE OF THE MARRIAGE	DEFERMENT
DEMONSTRATION	EMOTIONAL SIDE OF THE MARRIAGE	DENIAL
DETERMINATION	LIFE-CHOICES SIDE OF THE MARRIAGE	DEFENSIVENESS

What sort of a marriage do you really think you will end up with displaying Disinterest, Deferment, Denial, and Defensiveness? A marriage destined to fail will tragically eventuate.

A road and short cut passing through a very large out-back Canadian farm, connecting two main oft-used highways. It had a gate to be opened and then deliberately closed both ends of the 'road/short-cut,' when you drove through, protecting the cattle, but allowing you to gain access to the bypass farm road used as a short cut. On the gate was an interest sign. ***"Choose carefully which rut you go in, because you'll be in it for the next twenty miles."***

Out of the two lists in Figure 4. select carefully which list and attributes you will choose, as you're likely to experience the ultimate effect for many years to come.

Apologies To The Isaac Newton Purists

All of the historical facts about Isaac Newton in this work are totally accurate. For the environment of the story we have woven the fabric of other characters around Isaac. We have artificially created the 'Laws Of Relationship' as an alternate concept for the 'Laws Of Motion.' However, don't you think he could have really been writing about relationships?

Factual Identities

All characters within this work are fictitious. Any similarity to person or persons known is purely coincidental. However, all features expressed in the lives of the couples in the book have been experienced in a counselling environment. Each couple is an agglomeration of various couples and counselling situations.

Endnote

CONCLUSION OF RESOURCES TO FOOTNOTE 1.

[These continuing references clearly validate the inherent difficulties in de facto relationships and why marriage, though often not perfect, is a more stable relationship]

- Cohabitants tend not to be as committed as married couples, or prepared to work on their differences [1995 Journal of Family Issues]. Generally it is unusual for cohabitation to last more than 5 years.
- Particularly problematic is the area of serial cohabitation. It generates a greater willingness to dissolve later relationships [1993 Journal of Family Issues].
- About 60% of cohabitation end in marriage [1989 Australian National Study on Cohabitation].
- In general cohabiting relationships tend to be less satisfactory than married relationships, with cohabiting couples reporting lower levels of happiness, lower levels of sexual exclusivity and sexual satisfaction, and poorer relationships with parents [Bumpass, Sweet & Cherlin's 1991 study].
- Cohabitation has been consistently associated with poorer marital communications, lower marital satisfaction, higher levels of domestic violence, and great probability of divorce [Uni. Of Denver, Centre For Marital And Family Studies].
- After 5 years only 10% of cohabiting couples are together. De facto status does not tend to permanency. Consider effect upon children [Bumpass, Sweet's 1989 study].
- Married couples have substantial benefits over the unmarried cohabiters in terms of labour force productivity, physical and mental health, general happiness and longevity [1994 American Journal of Sociology].
- Annual rates of depression among cohabiting couples are more than 3 times the married rate [1990 Psychiatric Disorders in Australia].

- In cohabiting, physical and sexual abuse of female is much higher. One study showed twice as high, another study nearly three times [1991 Journal of Marriage and the Family].
- Abuse is 20 times higher for children with cohabiting, but biological parent/father, but 33 times greater if parent cohabiting with non-parenting/father male partner [1993 Family Education Trust: London].
- 1996 poverty rate was 6% with married parents, but 31% with cohabiting parents [1996 Journal of Marriage and the Family].
- Cohabiters have on average lower incomes and less education [1999 Social Forces].
- Australian National University found unmarried people need an income of $70,000 to display the same happiness as married person with income of only $20,000 [Australian Readers Digest May 1993].
- One of the annoying features for social therapists is that there is growing evidence that tax reforms make it beneficial to stay single, even if they try to hide it in cohabiting. This has been blamed for falling numbers of weddings [Daily Telegraphy, July 7th, 2007].
- Many cohabiting couples waste their young adulthood in relationships going nowhere [Weston, Qu: Aust. Institute Of Family Studies]. It may contribute to later pregnancies than personally desired and research has shown cohabitating relationships are becoming more unstable and less likely to lead to marriage [Melbourne Herald Sun Nov. 22, 2007].

From The Author

If you have enjoyed 'Marital Physics' we ask that you **recommend this book to all your friends** via your electronic Email database, Facebook, Twitter or whatever means you use to connect. You can advise them that they can procure 'Marital Physics' via:

Amazon.com

About The Author

Rev. Dr. Ivan Herald, along with his wife Pauline, has been in ministry for well over 45 years, working across a wide cross-section of church denominations, community, corporate, training institutes and government environments. Ivan, along with Pauline in 1989 founded a Not-For-Profit organisation, OzFAME [Australian **F**amily **A**nd **M**arriage **E**ducation].

Travelling nationally and internationally Ivan & Pauline speak on a wide range of topics in various settings, defined above. Over 100,000 have attended their full interactive 4-session Marriage/Relationship Seminar, with over 500,000 having attended single sessions in marriage, family, parenting, relationship, personal development (conflict and stress management etc) as well as business and corporate development.

Ivan and Pauline have authored 12 books and numerous programs in marriage, relationship, family, and business/leadership areas.

For 7 years they hosted their own cable-channel TV program 'Lifestyle Plus' on Australian cable channel. Ivan's Masters and Doctoral work major is in the 'Conflict Management' area.

Ivan has been awarded national recognition in 'Citizen Of The Year' in 'Community Services' at NSW Parliament House, because of his contribution to the quality of marriage, families and Australian community. A past Australian Prime Minister has personally commended Ivan and Pauline's work.

Ivan and Pauline are parents to three incredibly successful and amazing children and seven wonderful grandchildren.

For a list of Ivan/Pauline's books and an appraisal of their ministry go direct to: www.ozfame.com or

You Tube: link http://www.youtube.com/watch?v=fFd0P44dLBY

Direct contact with Ivan for any speaking or ministry enquiries can be made at: ivan@ozfame.com

www.ingramcontent.com/pod-product-compliance
Lightning Source LLC
Chambersburg PA
CBHW062203080426
42734CB00010B/1769